Enduring Grace

Quilts from the Shelburne Museum Collection
With Instructions for Five Heirloom Quilts

Celia Y. Oliver

C&T PUBLISHING

© 1997 Shelburne Museum

Editor: **Lee M. Jonsson**

Technical Editor: **Diana Roberts**

Copy Editor: **Judith M. Moretz**

Original Illustrations and Project Research: **Froncie Hoffhine Quinn**

Electronic Illustrations: **Lesley Gasparetti**

Book Design: **Lesley Gasparetti**

Cover Design: **John M. Cram and Kathy Lee**

All Quilt and Museum Photography: **Ken Burris**, Shelburne Museum,
    unless otherwise noted

Library of Congress Cataloging-in-Publication Data
Oliver, Celia Y.
    Enduring grace : quilts from the Shelburne Museum collection
  with instructions for five heirloom quilts / Celia Y. Oliver
        p.   cm.
    Includes bibliographical references and index.
    ISBN 1-57120-022-3
    1. Quilts--United States--History. 2. Quilts--Vermont-
  Shelburne Museum. I. Shelburne Museum.
  II. Title.
  NK9112.045 1997
  746.46'0973'0747435--DC21   96-44403
                                                          CIP

Published by C&T Publishing

P.O. Box 1456

Lafayette, CA 94549

Printed in China
10   9   8   7   6   5   4   3   2   1

TABLE OF CONTENTS

Enduring Grace

ELECTRA HAVEMEYER WEBB AND THE SHELBURNE MUSEUM

Electra H. Webb

The Shelburne Museum's collection of textiles includes quilts and other bedcovers, household textiles and furnishing fabrics, pictorial embroideries, decorative accessories, and costumes. Initially developed by the Museum's founder, Electra Havemeyer Webb, the collection has been recognized as one of the largest, broadest, and most diverse in the country.

Electra Webb had a great appreciation, in her words, for the "craftsmanship and ingenuity of our forefathers." Although she first began collecting quilts, furnishing fabrics, and other bedcovers as decorative accessories for her home, she soon began to regard them as works of art and documents of history. She assembled an exceptional collection which exhibited the depth and range of eighteenth- and nineteenth-century American bedcovers and the wide variety of fabrics, needlework, and printing techniques they represented. When the Shelburne Museum was founded in 1947, the bedcover collection numbered over 100, and by the time of Electra Webb's death in late 1960 it had grown to 400. Today the collection includes more than 700 examples of appliquéd, pieced, embroidered, paint-decorated, knit, crocheted, and hand-woven bedcovers.

Electra Webb was born in 1888, the third and youngest child of Louisine Elder and Henry O. Havemeyer, two of the most passionate and important collectors in America's Gilded Age.[1] They developed many diverse collections and are best known as collectors of European Old Master, nineteenth-century, and Impressionist paintings, Japanese wood-block prints, and Asian decorative arts. Electra Webb appreciated and acknowledged their influence. She wrote, "This early training, the living with and the looking at art of great beauty and variety, gave me a true appreciation of quality—and the desire to collect for myself."[2]

Electra Webb began collecting American art and antiques soon after her marriage to James Watson Webb in 1910. Inspired by the then-popular Colonial

Stencil House, Shelburne Museum.
From Columbus, New York, 1804.

Revival style, she furnished their houses in Shelburne, Vermont, and Westbury, Long Island, with country furniture and accessories. Samplers, lithographed landscapes, seascapes, and hunting prints were hung on walls covered with hand-printed and painted wallpapers. Transfer-printed ceramics, pewter, and stoneware pottery filled cupboards, tables, and mantels. Quilts, bedcovers, and other textiles were used on beds, chairs, and even lampshades, and hooked rugs covered the wooden plank floors. Electra Webb's passion for collecting continued throughout her years as a private collector and, if anything, increased during her career as founder, president, and chief curator of the Shelburne Museum.

When Electra Webb learned in 1947 that the Webb collection of twenty-eight horse-drawn vehicles would be sold, she saw her chance to realize a long-held dream to make her collections available to the public. She later wrote, "I couldn't bear to have these carriages go, so I said 'would you consider giving them to me if I had a little piece of property . . . in Shelburne where they could be seen by others. . . ?' [The Webb family agreed] . . . And that was

the start of the Shelburne Museum."[3] She purchased eight acres in Shelburne and the project was begun.

Electra Webb's priority was to build a museum to house and present her collections to the people of Vermont. She was inspired by other collectors and museum founders, including Henry Francis du Pont of Winterthur and Lawrence Rockefeller of Williamsburg; however, she had a strong desire to develop a museum that was different in concept and design from other outdoor museums. She explained her thoughts in a letter to Louis Jones, Director of the Museums at Cooperstown, New York. "Now, you ask me, what is the idea back of your museum?" she wrote ". . . I want it to be an educational project varied and alive, that will instill in those who visit it a deeper appreciation and understanding of our heritage. My thought is that it would depict the manner of living in Vermont and surrounding territories during the early days, and that the buildings and the collections housed therein would show the fine craftsmanship and the ingenuity of our forefathers."[4]

As the vision for her museum took shape, Webb focused her energy on collecting buildings and determining how best to exhibit her collections. One after another, historic buildings like the Dutton House in Cavendish, Vermont, and Stagecoach Inn in Charlotte, Vermont, were located and acquired, dismantled and moved to the museum, reconstructed, and filled with Electra Webb's collections. By 1950, six buildings were in progress. At the same time, she developed her long-range plan for the museum complex, which reflected her desire to present and interpret different aspects of community life in Vermont as well as the type of architecture used in the eighteenth and nineteenth centuries. Under Webb's direction her staff researched the history of each structure they acquired, and together they discussed where and how best to exhibit her collec-

Stencil House, Shelburne Museum. Electra Webb's first collection began as a child when her grandmother gave her six dolls.

tions. When the Shelburne Museum opened to the public in 1952, nine buildings, a unique combination of homes, community buildings, and galleries contained exhibits with over 9,000 objects.

As she designed her exhibits, Electra Webb presented her collections both as works of art and as utilitarian objects. This interest can be related to the early twentieth-century exhibitions and publications on folk art and handcrafts, and to such cultural art movements as Arts and Crafts, Art Nouveau, and Colonial Revival. These movements, although diverse, share an appreciation for the craftsmanship in the creation of utilitarian objects.

Electra Webb enjoyed the unusual and took particular delight combining objects —often unique, sometimes crude—which illustrated the creativity and ingenuity of the makers. Her view of everyday life in early- and mid-nineteenth century New England was portrayed in the historic houses and community buildings which created a contextual setting for the objects.

Working exhibits illustrated how artifacts were made, presenting the craftsperson, the tools, and finished objects. Domestic buildings were also used as galleries to exhibit entire collections of related objects. The Stencil House, a typical nineteenth-century farmhouse, actually serves as a gallery for the collection of paint-decorated furniture and accessories.

Electra Webb grouped objects such as quilts, dolls, tools, and folk sculpture in massive displays for the serious collector to study and enjoy. She understood the strong visual, emotional, and educational impact of exhibiting, for example, 1200 decoys in the Dorset House, a ten-room Greek Revival structure. These exhibits illustrate the same type of encyclopedic collecting that Electra Webb's father followed, acquiring objects in great numbers to reach beyond the norm, seeking out rare and unusual forms, as well as the most common.

When Shelburne Museum first opened, quilts, blankets, samplers, and other

Electra H. Webb

Appliquéd and Pieced Quilt, Arborescent Rose Tree Medallion Pattern. 1830. Made by Sarah T. C. Miller. Charleston, South Carolina. Cotton chintz, filled, quilted in crossed diagonals. 109" x 125". Museum acquisition 1969-053. (10-519)

Sarah Miller lived with her brother, Dr. Miller, the minister of the First Presbyterian Church. "Sis Sally," as she was known to her family and friends, never married and made this quilt for the guest room bed. Arborescent chintz fabrics were made in England for the American market and intended for use as bedcovers and bed hangings.

Florence Peto described and illustrated this quilt in her book *American Quilts and Coverlets*.

Florence Peto in her living room with some of her many quilts. The chintz Tree of Life quilt is now in the Shelburne collection (10-519). (Collection of Joyce Gross)

needlework were used as decorative accessories to furnish the historic houses. By 1954 visitors to the Hat and Fragrance Textile Gallery could walk through rooms filled with quilts and coverlets, rugs, samplers, costumes, hatboxes, and other needlework. This was the first time a major collection of textiles with such exceptional depth, range, and quality was made so immediately accessible to the public.

Many quilts and bedcovers were added to the collection between 1952 and 1960. Electra Webb purchased her antiques from antique dealers and private owners throughout the northeast. Business colleagues and friends were intrigued with her museum project and responded by locating, researching, and documenting artifacts for the collection. Electra Webb became acquainted with Florence Peto of New Jersey, the well-known author, lecturer, quiltmaker, and dealer in antique quilts. Her two books, *American Quilts and Coverlets* and *Historic Quilts*,[5] set a standard for historical research in the 1940s. Over the years Peto helped to develop and document the quilt collection, and in 1950 presented Webb with a copy of her book, *American Quilts and Coverlets*, and inscribed it, "To Electra Webb, with all good wishes for success in the project dear to her, Sincerely, Florence Peto." Peto worked closely with the Museum until Electra Webb's death in 1960 and acquired many exceptional quilts for the Museum collection, including the Mariner's Compass (10-22), the Arborescent Rose Tree Medallion (10-519), and Major Ringgold's Baltimore Album (10-330).

Electra Webb collected what she liked, what she said "spoke to me." The design motifs and subjects represented in the Museum's textile holdings relate strongly to the furniture, decorative arts, and folk sculpture also collected by Electra Webb throughout her life: geometric and curvilinear patterns, narrative and historical scenes, and designs based on combinations of floral motifs, human and animal figures,

Hatboxes, 1820-1850. Hat and Fragrance Textile Gallery, Shelburne Museum. (Photo: Ianthe Ruthven)

and unusual forms. She later wrote, "The same imaginative and creative quality appears in all the collections, and often the same motif, whether it appears on a carved object, a quilt, a rug, a chest, a sleigh, or a piece of pottery."[6]

Electra Webb also collected objects with highly decorated and embellished surfaces, whether they were painted, stenciled, quilted, printed, embroidered, glazed, or carved. This is evident when comparing her collections of printed fabric, bandboxes, lithographed prints, ceramics, carved and paint-decorated furniture, and many quilts and textiles with appliqué, quilting, embroidery, paint, and other surface decoration.

Electra Webb's interest in bold colors, strong geometric patterns, and graphic designs is reflected in the pieced quilts, hand-woven coverlets, and checked linens she collected. Balanced, symmetrical mosaic-like patterns also appear in her collections of paint-decorated furniture and accessories, all of which bear a strong resemblance to the wallpaper and stencil patterns used to decorate walls and bandboxes.

The geometric patterns contrast sharply with the elegant curvilinear patterns found on appliqué quilts, quilting patterns, embroidered blankets, and bed rugs. The serpentine vines and intertwined bird and floral forms found on rococo style furniture and decorative arts of the mid- to late-eighteenth century are echoed by the sinuous curves of eighteenth-century embroidery, block-printed resist textiles, paint decorated furniture, and decorative accessories also in the collection.

Floral-patterned bedcovers combined Electra Webb's interest in elegant, curvilinear and representational motifs. Examples range from medallion-style quilts with tree of life patterns or central floral wreaths to floral sprays and wreaths arranged in block-style grids, and single flower motifs scattered in an all-over pattern. Floral-patterned textiles in the study collection include clothing and furnishing fabric illustrating every type of eighteenth- and nineteenth-century printing technique: wood block, copperplate, and roller-printed textiles.

Electra Webb's interest in history and

Appliquéd Quilt, Tree of Life Pattern. 1800-1820. Made by Jeriesha Kelsey. Boston, Massachusetts. Cotton. 91" x 80". Museum acquisition 1990-12. (10-698)

everyday life led her to collect a wide variety of copperplate toile, block, and roller-printed yardage printed with detailed scenes. Quilts and bedhangings depict classical figures, farms and villages, historical figures and events, and architectural details. These bedcovers, when combined with her collection of historical prints, wallpaper panels, and over 200 bandboxes, provide a fascinating glimpse of American history.

Electra Webb once declared that she "tried to find the art in folk art,"[7] and admired artists who chose to include images of their everyday world in their work. She sought textiles which exemplified the ingenuity, creativity, and imagination of the maker, and assembled a group of quilts, embroidered blankets, jacquard coverlets, and textiles which featured unusual figures and forms. All relate strongly to the collections of folk sculpture, weathervanes, and whirligigs for which she was also well-

page 63

known. A crazy patchwork quilt made by Delphia Noice Haskins of Rochester, Vermont, featuring figures of men and women, and domestic, farm, and exotic animals appealed to Electra Webb. She later described it as ". . . rather amusing because [it is] so crude, [as if] the maker wanted to make it more decorative [so she] put in the animals and heads."[8]

The Museum's collections have continued to expand since Electra Webb's death in 1960, and the collection of bedcovers has almost doubled in size. Over the years, Museum staff have acquired quilts and other bedcovers which continue Electra Webb's collecting themes and, whenever possible, have a documented history of ownership. For example, the tree of life motif appears on quilts, embroidered blankets, and bed rugs as well as bedhangings, printed textiles, and samplers in the collections. To supplement these, the Museum acquired an appliqué quilt made in the

early 1800s by Jeriesha Kelsey of Boston, Massachusetts, depicting a variation of the tree of life motif surrounded by serpentine floral vines made with early block and roller-printed textiles (10-698). Also acquired was a late nineteenth-century silk quilt, appliquéd in a similar pattern, donated to the Museum by Sandra Todaro. The quilt was made in Chicago by a young woman who was trained in needlework in an Italian convent school (10-706). These two quilts are of particular interest because

Appliquéd Quilt, Tree of Life Pattern. 1880-1900. Made by an Italian immigrant woman. Chicago, Illinois. Silk. 116$\frac{1}{2}$" x 74$\frac{1}{2}$". Gift of Sandra Todaro 1987-51. (10-706)

they document the influence of rococo and baroque design on American and European textile traditions.

Since its beginning, the Museum has made a special effort to acquire exceptional Vermont objects. Recent acquisitions include two quilts from the Brush family of Jericho, Vermont; an 1810s wool quilt pieced in boldly-colored stripes and an 1840s cotton quilt pieced in a Flying Geese Medallion pattern.

page 50

page 61

Friends and family who supported Electra Webb as she built the Museum continue to donate important artifacts to the Museum's collection. Alice Winchester, a noted authority on American folk art and a great friend of Electra Webb, presented the Museum with a crazy quilt made by her grandmother, Catherine Mary Severance Winchester of Middlebury, Vermont, in the 1880s. Winchester, an accomplished artist, embellished the quilt with oil-painted landscapes, figures, and a whimsical frog playing a fiddle. The donor's brother, John Winchester, generously added to this important gift when he donated three other quilts, lace, and needlework all made by Catherine Winchester,

page 66

as well as the artist's paint box. The paint-decorated crazy quilt and paint box form an additional link to Shelburne Museum's collections of painted furniture and accessories.

Despite these recent acquisitions, the Museum has identified areas in the collection which needed to be strengthened in order to have a well-rounded collection. For example, we have focused attention on acquiring examples of quilts from the first decades of the twentieth century. A group of six floral appliqué quilts made by

Anna Baker of Ohio, in patterns and colors of the 1930s, were given to the Museum by Franklin Smith of St. Petersburg, Florida. These quilts provide an important interpretive link between nineteenth- and twentieth-century quiltmaking because the maker used both traditional and contemporary patterns for the quilts and rendered them in contemporary colors. These provide an interesting counterpoint to a stuffed white-work quilt made in 1931 by Bertha Meckstroth of Glencoe, Illinois, a sculptress turned quiltmaker. Meckstroth's original design of a bird plucking its breast is adapted from the medieval symbol for compassion, "A Pelican in its Piety." The quilt includes a verse worked in green reverse appliqué, "He shall cover thee with his feathers and under his wings shall thou trust" (10-723). Its acquisition complements the numerous nineteenth-century white-work quilts in the collection, as well as those which incorporate reverse appliqué and stuffed quilting.

page 73

Today the textile collections at Shelburne Museum continue to offer an unparalleled opportunity to view the breadth and depth of creativity that went into making American quilts and bedcovers. The quilts and bedcovers displayed on beds and cradles in the Museum's historic houses and exhibits in the Hat and Fragrance Textile Gallery are rotated annually and present the full range of bedcovers in the collection. Exhibits feature recent acquisitions as well as examples from Electra Webb's original collection. In recent years exhibits in the Hat and Fragrance Textile Gallery have been adapted to incorporate new conservation techniques, showcase new acquisitions, and provide enhanced interpretive context, while retaining much of Electra Webb's spirit and exhibit design style.

The collections of quilts and bed-

Catherine Mary Severance Winchester's paint box.

Bertha Meckstroth (Collection of Joyce Gross)

covers are researched, exhibited, and interpreted in many ways. When exhibited in the historic houses, they are interpreted as everyday objects which combine usefulness and beauty. When analyzed and researched as examples of folk art, they reveal patterns of decorative design and methods of production. And when combined with stenciled walls, painted furniture, stoneware pottery, pewter, and decorative textiles, they help create interiors notable for their distinctive profusion of colorful pattern and texture, and provide an introduction to the outstanding examples of pattern and design collected and highlighted by Electra Webb.

"9 woollen blankets, 4 bedquilts, 2 coverlids, 3 old coverlids, 2 blankets, 1 counterpane,

37 woollen blankets, 4 bed quilts, 1 calico bedquilt, and 2 old woollen blankets."

— Probate inventory, Salmon Dutton, 1824

AMERICAN QUILTS IN THE HOME

When Salmon F. Dutton, a wealthy land surveyor and store-keeper of Cavendish, Vermont, died in 1824, a probate inventory was prepared for his estate which documented his personal and household effects at the time of death. The number and variety of bedcovers and bedsteads, cloth yardage, and sewing, spinning, and weaving equipment in the house illustrates the manufacture and use of different types of bed covers in the nineteenth century.[1]

Quilts and other bedcovers have been made in America since early settlement days. Since that time, the style of quilts and attitudes toward them have been affected by a wide variety of influences. The textile goods available for quiltmaking and the technological advances in the textile industry certainly influenced the overall appearance and design of a quilt. But even more important were the social and cultural traditions of the maker's country of birth and the maker's contemporary cultural environment—the prevailing fashion for interior decorating styles and decorative arts, especially the design of wallpaper, carpets, and printed fabric.

Until the mid-nineteenth century, many of the textiles in the home were used for furnishing the bed, which consisted of the wooden "bedstead" (described as a four-posted bed fitted with either a rope or wooden slat bottom) and the bed "furniture" which consisted of the bed hangings, quilts or coverlets, blankets, sheets, pillow cases, and ticking.[2] *The Workwoman's Guide of 1838* provides instructions for furnishing a bed. The author recommends three mattresses or ticks, "the first made of straw, . . . The second made of horse hair or wool for large beds; and for children, of chaff, sea-weed, beech leaves, cocoa-nut fiber or paper, and many other things of that sort. The third mattress, known as the bed, bolster and pillows are filled with chicken, turkey, or goose feathers, and down, for the higher classes; and mill-puff, which is a kind of cotton, for the lower classes." Next came the bed linens: a bottom sheet, a long narrow bolster pillow which supported two smaller pillows, a top sheet, blankets, and crowning it all, a counterpane or coverlet. The

West bedchamber, Dutton House,
Shelburne Museum. From Cavendish, Vermont, 1782.

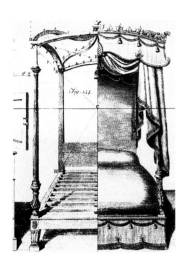

Four-post bed fitted with mattress, bedcover, and curtains.[3] (Winterthur Museum Library)

furnished bed was then fitted at the top and sides with curtains made from up to fifty yards of fabric. When closed at night, they created a warm, private environment, almost a room in itself. [4]

Homeowners often went to great expense to furnish the most important bed with elaborate bedcovers and curtains, which brought beauty, color, and design to the home and conveyed an element of status and wealth to visitors. Over the next three centuries, though circumstances changed, the best furnished bed in the house continued to connote the status of the household. So while today we focus a great deal of attention on individual quilts and coverlets, in their day they were part of an elaborate system of textiles which met practical, social, and aesthetic needs.

The quilts and other bedcovers which survive today, beautifully stitched whole cloth, pieced, and appliqué quilts made of imported wool, silk, and printed cotton, might lead us to believe that these were the only types of quilts made at that time. However, it is important to look beyond the examples which remain. The quilts which survive in private and public collections are only a small sampling of a much larger number made and used in early America. Written references and illustrations provide an indication of the use and prevalence of quilted bedcovers. Typically, only the best quilts and bedcovers in a household were protected and preserved. Everyday quilts were used up in their function as utilitarian objects.

The collection of over seven-hundred bedcovers at the Shelburne Museum highlights the wide range of textiles made in New England and northeastern America, and chronicles the manufacture and use of quilts, coverlets, and embroidered bedcovers from the eighteenth through the twentieth century. Other collections of domestic and imported textiles, such as furnishing fabrics, bed hangings, carpets, and table covers, as well as the collections of decorative arts and needlework, provide an interpretive context for the bed covers.[5]

Textiles in Colonial America

The early settlers of New England, Virginia, the Carolinas, and New Amsterdam were able to bring few household possessions with them from their European homes. Textiles however, especially clothing and bedding, were among the items that colonists were advised to bring on the initial voyage. In 1681 William Penn wrote a treatise, *A* *Brief Account of the Province of Pennsylvania*, to invite settlers to his colony and provide practical advice about the work involved in settling a colony. He wrote, "But they that go must widely count the Cost, For they must work themselves, or be able to employ others. A Winter goes before a Summer, and the first work will be Countrey Labour: to clear Ground, and

East bedchamber, Prentis House, Shelburne Museum. From Hadley, Massachusetts, 1773. Wool whole cloth quilt (1780-1800); curtains of resist-dyed cotton.

While the straw tickings needed to be refilled with clean straw as it crushed and flattened, feather beds or mattresses had more lasting value and often received special attention in probate inventories. Appraisers recorded the type of feathers: pigeon, goose, etc., and even "live" or "dead."

raise Provision; other things by degrees. . . . The Goods fit to take with them for use or sale are all Utensils for Husbandry and Building, and Household-stuff; Also all sorts of things for Apparel, as Cloath, Stuffes, Linnen &c."6

Textiles were essential for warmth and comfort, and were more easily packed and transported on a ship than other household goods. Also, clothing and bed furnishings were expensive, valuable commodities, and manufacturing new goods required considerable time, expertise, and a large supply of raw materials—none of which were readily available in the wild, undeveloped colonies.

The bed, quilts, and bed hangings served multiple purposes in the earliest days. Homes were small and sparsely furnished, many containing only one or two rooms and a loft. Consequently, each room served several functions, and beds shared space with tables, chairs, and cupboards.

Even in the homes of the wealthy, the best bed was often placed in the parlor where socializing and entertaining took place. The bed furnishings provided warmth in poorly heated houses, and privacy in bedchambers that might accommodate four to six people.

Textiles were an essential part of every household inventory and constituted a greater part of a family's wealth than they do today. Time consuming to produce and expensive to acquire, they consequently were prized as valuable commodities and treated with great care. The bedstead, bed linens, and furnishing fabrics were often itemized separately in probate inventories and listed immediately after land holdings, livestock, money, and silver, an indication of their importance as an asset in evaluating a family's relative worth. This remained true through the early 1800s.

Domestic and Imported Cloth—Eighteenth Century

Benjamin Church's advertisement in the March 12, 1770 *Boston Gazette and Country Journal.*

Hannah Hickok Smith of Connecticut wrote to her mother in 1800 describing the activity of her five daughters, "The girls ... have been very busy spinning this spring and have spun enough for about seventy yards besides almost enough for another carpet."[7]

Before the industrial revolution mechanized the production of cloth in the early nineteenth century, all types of wool, silk, and cotton cloth and thread, whether imported or domestic, were made by hand. While colonists acquired many of their household goods from Europe, they also brought a wealth of traditions and handicraft skills from their mother country, which enabled them to produce some of the goods needed in the colonies. The making of quilts and quilted articles was based on centuries of production and use in the British Isles and Continental Europe.[8] The clothing, bedding, household textiles, and decorative accessories the colonists brought to America were the physical representations of those traditions that would provide a lasting reminder and visual reference.

Plain and checked wool and linen fabrics were considered suitable for everyday clothing, toweling, and bedding. Many colonial households relied on locally produced cloth for their basic household textiles. However, there was no large-scale textile industry in the American colonies as there was in England and the European countries. The output of a typical hand weaver in the colonies could not compete with the amount, variety, and cost of English and European goods available from local merchants. In Rowley, Massachusetts, in the 1670s, the most productive weaver in the community processed less cloth in ten years than one Boston merchant received in one shipment from England.[9]

Most of the cloth used for better quality clothing, bedding, and bed furniture was imported from abroad. Expensive wool, silk, and cotton goods were shipped from England and France, delivered to ports along the eastern coast including Boston, Providence, New York, Philadelphia, Baltimore, and Charleston, and distributed through local merchants. Merchants advertised available goods in local newspapers and carried sample books and trade cards from London manufacturers which featured such fabrics as checked camlets; serge; plain, striped, or checked linen; and luxurious figured velvets for buyers to examine and order.[10] In 1766 Norfolk, Virginia, merchants Balfour and Barroud advertised India chintz; calico; printed linens and cottons; sprig linen; flowered, plain, and striped dimities; Marseilles quilting; and ready made counterpanes.[11] Textiles were also purchased at public "vendue" or auction. The September 16, 1782, edition of a Boston paper, *The Independent Ledger and American Advertiser*, contained a notice in the "Sales by Auction" column posted by William Greenleaf that he would sell "by PUBLIC VENDUE . . . a general assortment of piece goods, among which are . . . chintzes, calicoes, figured velvets, . . . [and] a great variety of striped and checked cottons."[12]

By the mid-1700s, however, the constant demand for textiles, the high cost of imported goods, the erratic shipments from England, a desire for independence from the British mercantile system, and a general frustration at the economic stronghold of English taxes and restrictions on American manufacturing efforts provided the impetus for colonists to increase the home production of textiles.

Each person in a household, by necessity, took part in some aspect of textile production. Farmers in rural areas maintained small flocks both for mutton and wool, and in some cities common land was provided for grazing cows and sheep. Wool from the annual shearing was sorted, picked clean, washed, and carded, a process which extended over many months. Flax grown for the production of linen cloth required eighteen months of intensive labor from planting to harvest to preparing the fiber for spinning. In some areas, raw cotton grown in the West Indian Islands was also available for spinning. Every female was taught at an early age the essential skills of spinning, sewing, and knitting. Throughout their lives they would spend part of each day in some aspect of textile production.

Wool, cotton, and linen fibers were spun into thread for knitting or weaving clothing, bedding, blankets, bedcovers, towels, table linens, and even sacks. Ruth Henshaw Bascomb of Derry, New Hampshire, kept a journal through much of her life and recorded the daily activities of her family, including spinning wool for aprons, linen for shirting, and cotton for shirting, stockings, and fringe.[13] Relatively few women, however, were taught to weave. New England inventories reveal that while virtually every household, however small, had at least one spinning wheel, less than one household in ten contained a loom or other weaving equipment. Weaving required special training and technical expertise; these skills were often passed through a family or to an apprentice.

Many families bartered with local weavers for cloth. Samuel and Mary Lane of Stratham, New Hampshire provided each of their five daughters a generous supply of goods and furniture to set up housekeeping. His account book contains detailed lists of the furnishings provided to each daughter when she married, and reveals much about the process of acquiring textiles in the eighteenth century. Before his eldest daughter Mary was married in 1762 to John Crocket, Lane commissioned local people to provide household textiles. Samuel Allen was paid for weaving "coverlids," Daniel Allen's wife for weaving blankets, and Lydia Nokes for weaving 13½ yards of ticking. A sum of 14 pounds was recorded in Lane's account book as the payment to Mary Haley for "Quilting a Bed Quilt."[14]

Once the cloth was acquired, women could apply their needlework skills to the production of clothes, household linens, quilts, bedcovers, and other essential articles. Probate inventories in the seventeenth and eighteenth centuries revealed a wide variety of bedcovers in use: blankets, bed rugs, and coverlets made of cotton, linen, wool, rag and even hair; counterpanes; and pieced and whole cloth (also called plain) bed quilts.[15] An extensive group of textiles made, purchased, and used by the Copp family of Stonington, Connecticut, documents the variety of goods used in New England in the late 1700s and early 1800s. This rare collection, presented to the Smithsonian Institution in the 1890s, includes quilts, counterpanes, blankets, coverlets, bed hangings and furniture, table linens, towels, bolts of linen yardage, and costume items.

Barnframe loom, Vermont, 1800-1820.

Design Influences in the Eighteenth Century

Sr. Timy Thicketts first Reel to London or the Beauties of Kings Place drawing Lots . . . London, Printed for R. Sayer and J. Bennett, 1781. The bed hangings and bedcover, trimmed with ornamental braid and fringe, appear to be made with sprigged cotton. (Lewis Walpole Library, Yale University)

Detail. Whole Cloth and Embroidered Counterpane, Vermicelli Pattern. 1725-1750. Owned by the Almy family. South Dartmouth and New Bedford, Massachusetts. Linen, silk thread. 106" x 87". Gift of Electra Webb Bostwick 1954-526. (10-120)

The same design motifs which embellished textiles were also used on furniture, decorative accessories, everyday utensils, book covers, and gravestones. A quilt in the Shelburne collection dating from the early 1700s descended through the Almy family of South Dartmouth and New Bedford, Massachusetts. The closely-worked foliate designs embroidered in yellow silk thread on a plain linen ground resemble the carvings on this chest over drawers from the Hadley area of Massachusetts.

During the eighteenth century the designs and patterns used in American bedcovers were strongly influenced by English, European, and Asian textiles and decorative accessories. There were three major stylistic influences during this century: the baroque, rococo, and neoclassic styles. In the early 1700s decorative design was dominated by the baroque style, which had been introduced to England by Charles II and his Portuguese wife in the 1600s. Furniture and other utilitarian objects were embellished with carved and painted squares, rectangles, or diamonds, then filled with

geometric motifs, "C" scrolls, and curled foliate designs. The rococo style which developed from the baroque was a major influence on decorative arts and design in the 1700s. This lighthearted style is characterized by a constant use of curved line and such decorative motifs as scallop shells, ribbons, and "S" scrolls, and such classical motifs as urns and foliate forms in asymmetrical patterns. Classical motifs, first adapted by European Renaissance designers from Roman art, began to appear at this time. Popular motifs included Roman arches, Doric columns, acanthus leaves, urns, and baskets of flowers.

Many American needleworkers understandably relied on textiles brought from their home country as a source of design. Numerous eighteenth-century English and European quilts are largely designed as whole cloth quilts of white or colored cloth embellished with elaborate quilting and/or embroidery stitches. Elegant woven fabrics made in England and France served as one of the primary sources for textiles, as women incorporated the designs in embroidery and quilt patterns. Quilted bed covers of all types were made and decorated with embroidery, appliqué, and patchwork of geometric and floral patterns. It is likely that women shared their patterns and techniques with family and friends, often working together on quilting projects.[16]

American merchants, cabinetmakers, upholsterers, and consumers kept themselves informed about the latest trends for textile colors and patterns used in English and European bedchambers, just as quilters today study magazine and book illustrations for their design inspiration. Such well-known artists as William Hogarth and Thomas Rowlandson incorporated parlors and bedchambers in their prints, paying careful attention to descriptive details of furnishing fabrics.

The most fashionable bedchambers in New England were outfitted with solid colored bed furnishings often made from costly imported wool fabric. Whole cloth quilts made to coordinate with bed hangings and curtains were popular throughout New England from the early 1700s through the early 1800s. These quilts, made from one type of cloth, either plain or printed, were often quilted in geometric or floral designs. Especially popular was a high-quality imported glazed worsted wool in dark tones of blue, brown, red, rose, and even orange.

The earliest documented whole cloth quilt of this type in the Shelburne Museum collection was made of cerise-colored glazed wool by Abigail Livermore Keyes in 1762 for her brother, Jonathan Livermore of Wilton, New Hampshire. Lined with mauve-colored glazed wool and quilted in swirling acanthus leaf scrolls, this bedcover illustrates the most elegant type of wool quilt made at this time. The symmetrically central "S" scroll pattern strongly resembles the decorative scrollwork used in the rococo style for wood carving and metal work. While family tradition attributes this quilt to Abigail Livermore, it is also possible this quilt was made in England for the American market, and commissioned by the Livermores. Merchants and well-to-do homeowners often acquired ready-made quilts of copperplate-printed cottons as well as silks and plaid or striped Irish linen. In 1760 John Baylor of Newcastle, Virginia, ordered "two bedd quilts" and "two Redd Sarcenett Quilted Petticoats" from London merchants Flowerdeau & Norton.[17]

Green was a popular color, considered "very refreshing to the eye," and was often recommended for bedchamber furnishings. When Sarah Anna Emery wrote her biography in the 1870s, she reminisced about her grandmother's bed, hung with green moreen curtains trimmed with heavy gimp, in a contrasting color, which added to the visual effect.[18] A quilt in the Shelburne collection likewise reflects the popularity of this color. In 1800 Melinda Brown of Corinth, Vermont, purchased imported glazed worsted wool cloth to make her own quilt. She backed it with a hand-woven plain weave blanket, stuffed it with carded wool, and quilted the layers together.

More modest American homes furnished their bedchambers with striped, plaid, and checked linen and wool fabric or plain white corded cotton. Henry Wansey

Detail. Whole Cloth Quilt, The Farewell Party Pattern. 1820-1840. Made by Mrs. Dutton. Wilmington, Connecticut. Cotton. 90" x 76". Gift of Mrs. Charles E. Wilson 1954-526. (10-131)[19]

Detail. Whole Cloth Quilt, Floral Quilted Pattern. 1769. Made by Abigail Livermore Keyes (1721-1801). Wilton, New Hampshire. Glazed wool. 104" x 98". Museum acquisition 1987-38.[20] (10-656)

Dressing table, Connecticut, 1750-1790. The carved shells and bold "S" curves repeated in the skirt and cabriole legs are typical of the rococo style.

West bedchamber, Prentis House, Shelburne Museum. From Hadley, Massachusetts, 1773. Wool whole cloth quilt (1760-1780); embroidered linen bed curtains, (1750-1780). The popularity of printed cottons inspired many women to embroider patterns on bedcovers and curtains. Flowers, trees, and exotic animals were worked in brightly colored wool yarn on creamy wool, linen, or cotton cloth which would be displayed on the best bed. The bed curtains in Joseph Lee's eighteenth-century home in Cambridge, Massachusetts were described by Dorothy Dudley in her diary as "all worked in gorgeous colored worsteds by … Mrs. Lee … with gay figures of birds perched on trees scarcely larger than themselves."[21] Embroidered bedcovers continued to be popular throughout the 1800s, but were made in fewer numbers than appliqué or pieced quilts.

in his 1794 account of his travels in America commented on seeing checked bed hangings and window curtains in a Norwich, Connecticut, house, a reference which is matched by an inventory of the Avery home in Norwich which lists "six check'd window curtains." Wansey wrote, "At one house where I stopped, a young woman told me that … the checked window curtains were her own making, of flax raised, dressed, and spun by herself and sister, as well as the bed furniture of the house."[22]

In the mid-1700s the fashion for bed hangings made of solid colored wool fabric and linen, and cotton "furniture checks," declined due to the increased availability of block-printed chintz fabrics and the introduction of copperplate printed fabrics. Their figured and floral patterns transformed the appearance of the entire house, especially the bedchamber. George Hepplewhite, author of the highly regarded book *The Cabinet-maker and Upholsterer's Guide* (published in 1788, 1789, and 1794), recommended the use of cotton fabric for furniture, especially white dimity, printed cotton, and linen.[23] Harriet Beecher

Stowe recalled a fold-up bed in her Aunt Esther's parlor which was "concealed in the daytime by a decorous fall of chintz drapery."[24] The earliest chintz fabrics were imported from India, but less expensive English and French versions soon appeared on the market. Cotton bed hangings and furnishing yardage in the Shelburne Museum's collection document the availability and popularity of fabric embellished with exotic flowers and birds which were often copied from popular botanical prints and floral needlework patterns.

Copperplate prints revolutionized textile printing. The fine lines of the engraved metal plates allowed designers to create far more detailed scenes than could be produced with wood-block printing. Ben Franklin documented the popularity of these exotic prints when he wrote his

page 50

wife from London in 1758, "There are also 56 yards of cotton, printed curiously from copper plates, a new invention, to make bed and window curtains, and seven yards of chair bottoms printed in the same way, very neat."[25]

New cotton fabrics printed with landscape and narrative scenes were also used for quilts, bed hangings, and window curtains. Designers, like J. B. Huet of the Oberkampf textile factory in Jouy, France, became famous for the production of engraved plates with scenes depicting everyday life, hunting, history, and popular historical and fictional characters. In 1765 Richard Bancker, a dry goods merchant, offered "red, blue, and purple copperplate furniture, calicoes, and chintz furniture."[26]

Textiles imported from France were widely available in America throughout the 1700s. Many French cities and towns had long been famous for the elaborate woven and printed goods they produced. Textile manufacturers in Marseilles established trade with the American colonies in the 1600s, exporting cotton and silk fabrics

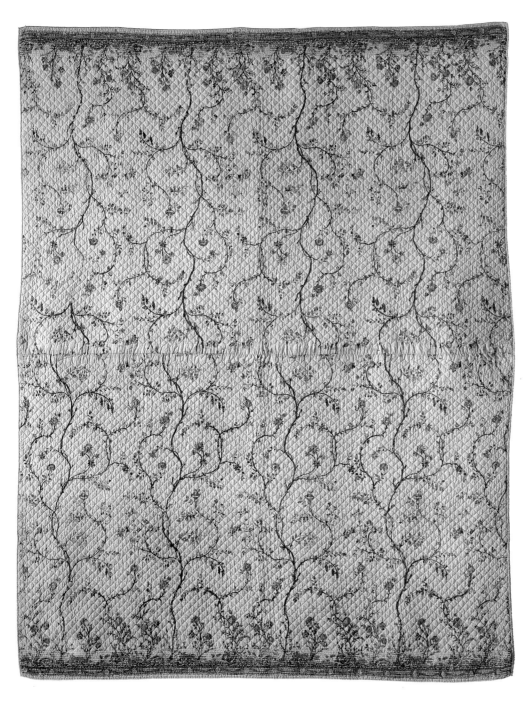

The rose vines resemble the "S"
scrolls typical of the rococo style.
Striped quilting along the border
was often used in Marseilles
quilting.

This quilt in the Shelburne
Museum collection, made of a floral printed cotton fabric, features
the puffed diamond quilting pattern and corded border typical of
the Marseilles goods.[27] The quilted
textile was originally made as a
petticoat in the mid-1700s. However, when the fashion for heavily-
quilted petticoats waned in the
early 1800s, the garment was
made over for use as a quilt; the
fabric was cut in half, the gathering
let out, and the two pieces sewn
together along the former waist.

quilted as bedcovers, clothing, and yardage.
Merchants from Norfolk and Williamsburg,
Virginia, advertised Marseilles quilting and
ready-made counterpanes for sale with
their other textiles.

Piecework quilts made in late eigh-
teenth- and early nineteenth-century
America were undoubtedly patterned after
their English and European counterparts.
The extant eighteenth-century English
pieced and appliquéd quilts feature floral
and geometric patterns arranged in a central medallion framed with a series of borders. A pieced medallion-style quilt made
by Mary (Dingee) Priestley (1767-1852)
of Ossining, New York,
in the late eighteenth or
early nineteenth century
illustrates the influence
of English piecework
quilting in American
needlework. The Dingee family emigrated

page 44

Detail. Embroidered linen bed curtains, Prentis House.

Check and plaid fabrics were used for tickings, bedcovers, curtains, and upholstery throughout the late 1700s and mid-1800s.

from England some time after Mary's birth. Undoubtedly the tradition of piece-work quilting was taught to Mary by her mother. Patchwork quilts designed in the central medallion style, with patterns composed of squares, triangles, diamonds, and hexagons, were popular in England in the 1700s.[28] Family tradition relates that Mary pieced this quilt using fabric from clothing belonging to her family and her own trousseau clothes made from fabric purchased in Philadelphia.[29] Between 1774 and 1800 numerous cloth weavers and dyers were in operation in that city, as well as eleven copperplate printers and seventeen calico printers, the two best known being John Hewson and Walters and Bed-well. In the last quarter of the eighteenth century Philadelphia was considered the center of America's textile industry.[30]

Industrialization of Textiles

The introduction of carding mills in the 1790s virtually eliminated the labor inten-sive task of hand carding for the home spinner. Fulling mills established at the same time made it easier to pro-cess finished woolen cloth. These two innovations com-bined to simplify the pro-duction of woolen yarn and cloth for hand weavers.[31]

The American textile industry benefited from technological developments in England. In 1790 Samuel Slater introduced power-driven machinery for spinning cotton thread in Rhode Island. The tech-nology quickly spread throughout New England, resulting in the ready availability of inexpensive factory-spun yarn.[32] Joseph Hough & Company, a general store and dry goods establishment, advertised in 1818 that they carried, "in addition to their general assortment of goods, cotton yarn of various numbers . . . at a discount . . . from the established factory prices."[33] Spinning mills and dry goods merchants often contracted with domestic hand weavers to weave cotton cloth. The *Middlebury [Vermont] National Standard* car-ried the following advertisement, "wanted immediately a number of good women weavers—apply to David Page, Jr."[34] Mill owners also provided space for professional weavers in the mills. Leonard Dakin advertised that he was available to produce "carpets and coverlets" in the factory owned by the Middlebury [Vermont] Manufacturing Company.[35] The cloth printing industry also benefited from the production of machine-spun yarn because the weavers could now produce more

cloth to be printed. But for all the new available cotton yarn, American weavers still could not compete with the long-established and powerful English mercan-tile system.

In the late eighteenth and early nine-teenth centuries, virtually every commu-nity in the northeast with a waterway or millpond could boast of a carding mill for the processing of raw wool, and a fulling mill for finishing wool cloth. As produc-tion of wool cloth suitable for clothing, bedcovers, bed hangings, and curtains became more efficient and less expensive, it was more affordable for a wider group of people.

Many women, freed from the time-consuming tasks of carding and spinning thread, had more time to care for their families, tend their homes, and make dec-orative utilitarian household objects. Each bedchamber was provided with blankets, coverlets, pieced and appliquéd quilts, or embroidered bedcovers, although not all were furnished in the best and most fash-ionable style. The number of quilts made in the mid-nineteenth century which have survived is an indication of the increased popularity of quiltmaking as well as the increased amount of leisure time available to some women.

Palampores and Appliqué Quilts

In the late 1700s and early 1800s, Indian printed cotton shawls, lengths of fabric (panels), bedspreads called "palampores," and finished quilts, decorated with popular flowers, plants, trees, or exotic birds, were widely available in America.[36] Women used the printed fabric for clothing and bed furniture, while the printed bedspreads were also made into quilts. Ruth Henshaw Bascomb of Derry, New Hampshire, described in her journal how "a printed India cotton coverlet had to have a backing made for it, then must be quilted."[37]

Historically, printed and woven textiles influenced the patterns used in embroidery and needlework designs. Consequently it was not unusual for the designs and patterns used on these eighteenth-century imported textiles to be a strong influence in the development and design of appliqué quilts in America. The

page 48

appliqué technique allows the maker great flexibility in creating a pattern, as individual motifs are cut from printed or plain fabric, then "laid on" and sewn to a plain cloth ground. It is likely that printed cloth was often purchased to make a new quilt, as the color and patterns were important for the completion of the design. The motifs used on the Indian cloth were arranged in essentially two ways—as an all-over pattern with the elements scattered across the surface or in a central medallion format. Women were inspired by the designs to create appliqué bedcovers, often in direct imitation of the original fabric.

page 48

page 49

page 49

Palampores are coverlets composed of one or two printed chintz panels; the term was first used in East India Company records in 1614.

Post-Revolutionary and Early Nineteenth-Century America

In the years following the Revolution, economic and political stability brought prosperity to a rising middle class in America. Increased wealth was manifested in part by new house styles with more elaborate floor plans. In place of general purpose rooms, spaces were now furnished for specific functions. Sitting rooms and parlors were located on the ground floor, with the bedchambers upstairs.

During the late 1700s the neoclassical style of decorating became all-important in American design. Incorporating architectural forms and decorative elements from Greece, the oldest democracy on earth, into American architecture, furniture design,

wallpaper, clothing, and textiles seemed the perfect way for Americans to express the ideals of their new democracy. Two experiences influenced this revival of classical antiquity—the rediscovery of Greek art as the original source of classical style, and the excavations of Herculaneum and Pompeii, which for the first time revealed the daily life of the ancients and the full range of their arts and crafts. Illustrated books depicting classical architecture made the art, architecture, and archeology of ancient Greece and Rome more widely available, even to Americans unable to travel, and helped inspire the neoclassical movement. One of the earliest books on the subject, *Classical Antiquities of Athens,*

Console table with marble top. Boston, Massachusetts, 1780-1800. Flowers and fruit decorating the apron in paint and gilt were probably derived from an English source book.

Whole Cloth Quilt, Neoclassical Temple Scene. 1825-1840. Maker unknown. Starksboro, Vermont. Cotton. 96" x 89". 1955-656. (10-168)

published by James Stuart and Nicolas Revett in 1762, and again in 1789, included measured drawings and commentary on design and construction techniques.[38]

Soon such noteworthy English architects as Robert Adams began to use elements of Greek architecture in their designs. Adams also wrote two books which proved to be a major influence on the revival of classical tastes.[39] In 1812 George Smith published *A Collection of Ornamental Designs After the Manner of the Antique*, one of the first affordable publications, which illustrated and introduced classical designs to a large number of people. Educated Americans acquired books on archeology as well as design books which featured suitable decorative motifs for the neoclassical interior. The Ridgely family of Hampton, Maryland, north of Baltimore, is known to have owned a copy of Smith's design book as well as a book by the French designer Pierre de La Mésangere.[40]

By the 1820s neoclassical motifs and design elements were widely adapted into vernacular decorating styles. Motifs introduced and used extensively in textiles, furniture, and other decorative arts by designers and cabinetmakers included acanthus and laurel leaves, baskets, wreaths,

and garlands of flowers, urns, and shields. Eagles became especially popular, both as a symbol of Rome and of the new nation. Classical designs became increasingly elaborate with the addition of stenciling, gilding, veneer, and carved figures.

Bedcovers, wallpapers, and furnishing fabrics in the Shelburne collection illustrate the influence of the neoclassical style, featuring motifs based on Greek and Roman wall paintings and frescoes. Wallpapers used at this time illustrate the use of octagons and other decorative architectural devices to frame decorative motifs and figural scenes. A copperplate-printed cotton bed hanging fragment which features these framing devices closely resembles a textile designed by J. B. Huet of France c. 1800. The popularity of this style is further illus-

page 47

trated by the appliquéd counterpane made by a member of the Spaulding family of Townsend Harbor, Massachusetts, c. 1820, which features figural scenes and flowers cut from block and copperplate-printed fabrics set in octagon-shaped frames.

Following the War of 1812, English manufacturers took advantage of the resumption of trade and flooded the American market with printed cotton goods. While the increased availability of wool, silk, and printed cotton goods was a boon to consumers, the competition from the distributors of imported textiles put added pressure on the still growing American textile industry.

Small-scale prints stamped in a bright palette of madder and azure blue and the green/brown/yellow-gold so-called "drab" palette were fashionable from the early 1800s through 1820s. This cloth was extensively printed by Jonathan Peel at his printworks at Church Bank, Lancashire, and by his brother Joseph Peel at the family's Bury, England, printworks.[41] An appliquéd counterpane in the Shelburne collection, made by Ann Robinson, probably from New England, dated 1813, illustrates the use of these imported English textiles in American quilts. Robinson

page 45

incorporated a flower-filled cornucopia and laurel leaf medallion with the Tree of Life motif, a popular design which was largely inspired by Indian textiles and used frequently in American needlework. The inclusion of animals running along small hills closely relates to embroidered samplers made at the same time.

English and French printworks also continued to produce floral chintz fabrics which featured classical designs. Quilters in the mid-Atlantic and southern states used these textiles to produce elegant appliqué counterpanes made in the central medallion style. Many of the appliqué quilts and counterpanes made by southern quilters incorporate floral printed arborescent chintz fabrics designed in the rococo style.[42] A quilt in the Shelburne collection illustrates the delicacy achieved by many southern quilters, especially those in Virginia. Both the Robinson and Virginia counterpanes feature the central medallion style—a central motif framed either by concentric diamonds and squares or by multiple borders.

page 52

By the late 1820s the American textile industry was fully mechanized with power-driven equipment for spinning, weaving, and printing cloth. Mechanized textile production dramatically changed the type and quantity of yarn and cloth available to the consumer. The Merrimack Manufacturing Company in Lowell, Massachusetts, was one of the first mill complexes developed with the capability of processing raw cotton into finished cloth. By 1826 more than 135 cotton factories in Massachusetts outfitted with power looms were producing over 60,000 yards of fabric per week, including sheeting, shirting, toweling, and clothing yardage in plain, striped, checked, and brightly printed cottons.[43]

Manufacturers lost no time making these mass-produced and inexpensive textiles available to consumers. General stores and dry goods establishments advertised a variety of American-made textiles as well as the more expensive imported goods. A dry goods supplier in Middlebury, Vermont, placed the following advertisement in the November 28, 1828 *National Standard*: "N. Wood & Co. has just received a fresh supply of English, India and American goods . . . including Superfine American Broad clothe (very cheap) of several colors, power loom and American shirtings."[44]

Quilters were quick to take advantage of these inexpensive factory-woven goods for their sewing needs. Quilting became

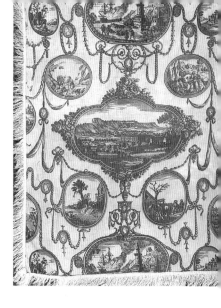

Curtain fragment used by the Strong family of Shelburne, Vermont (1800-1810). The neoclassical scenes originally printed in purple have faded to brown. (11-351)

Left: Calico printing by hand, Engraving. "Facing Calico Printing." Plate XII, engraved for supplement to *The Gentlemen's Magazine*, London, Hinton, 1749. (Collection of Museum of American Textile History)
Right: Calico printing machine, *Memoir of Samuel Slater* by George S. White, 1836.

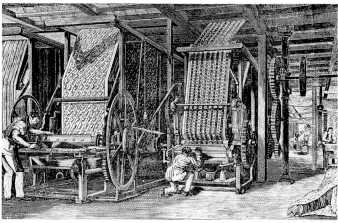

Tuckaway General Store,
Shelburne Museum.

more popular than ever before. Sarah Johnson, a quilter in Lancaster County, Pennsylvania, included over forty different cotton prints in a medallion star quilt which she marked with her initials and the date, 1826.

page 93

The Chintz appliqué medallion quilt dated 1830 made by Sarah T. C. Miller of South Carolina incorporates elaborately colored and detailed chintz fabrics probably purchased for this quilt. Arborescent chintz fabrics, featuring exuberant blooming 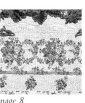 bushes and floral sprays, were widely used by quilters in the 1830s and 1840s. The flowering tree featured in this medallion style quilt is reminiscent of the Tree of Life image used

page 8

in appliquéd counterpanes made in the previous century.

Meanwhile, other quiltmakers continued to make everyday quilts pieced of scraps saved from various sewing projects, or clothing no longer in fashion or too worn for daily use. A Nine and Four Patch quilt made of various printed cottons descended through the Brock family of Newbury, Vermont. Harriet Brock, a maiden lady, is believed to be the maker of this quilt. The quilt pieces, ranging in size from one to four inches, include block and copperplate textiles dating from the late eighteenth century as well as cotton fabrics manufactured in the first quarter of the nineteenth century.

page 52

The Victorian Style in the Mid-Nineteenth Century

The industrial revolution of the early and mid-nineteenth century, centered first in the textile industry, was quickly adapted to mechanize other industries, including printing, iron casting, firearms, and transportation. The growth and increased production resulted in a strong American economy and a larger, more widely-based, middle class consisting of merchants, mechanics, shopkeepers, machinists, and mill managers. These economic changes also created new domestic roles for women. Content to rely on factory-woven goods for their everyday textile needs, women focused their creative talents on decorative needlework, especially quilting.

By the 1830s Victorian architecture and decorative styles had begun to influence American taste. Queen Victoria reigned from 1837 to 1901. During that time twenty American presidents, Andrew Jackson to Theodore Roosevelt, were in office, and enormous changes took place in American culture—social values, political and economic stability, and national pride. The Victorian period, which actually consisted of three separate time periods, early (1830-1850), middle (1850-1870), and late (1870-1890), was influenced by three distinct romantic revival movements. The Gothic revival style emphasized vertical lines and spirituality. The rococo revival style focused on elegant curvilinear lines, as

Appliquéd and Embroidered Counterpane, Floral Diamond Medallion. 1854. Made by Mary Jane Carr. Lancaster, Pennsylvania. Cotton, velvet. 92" x 99". Museum acquisition 1958. (10-327)

The central medallion style regained popularity in the mid-1800s. This quilter used brightly colored solid cotton fabrics for her appliqué quilt, which incorporates a central medallion of figural and floral motifs framed by flowering vines.

Genealogical information received with this quilt when it was acquired said that it was made by an ancestor of the Slade family of Lancaster, Pennsylvania. Research revealed that two adults named Mary Carr, one age sixty and the other age twenty-three, resided in Lancaster at the time of the 1850 census. The elder Mary Carr was born in Ireland in 1790. At age sixty she was living in Lancaster with her son Patrick, age fourteen, who was also born in Ireland. The workmanship in this quilt and its sophisticated pattern would indicate that it was the work of an experienced, skilled seamstress.

well as an interest in nature and the wilderness. The classical revival style emphasized an increased use of ancient Greek and Roman motifs as decorative symbols. These three styles existed simultaneously throughout the Victorian period, and although one might briefly take precedence over the others, designers often combined them to create a unique, eclectic, and sometimes confusing decorative collage.

Victorian architecture was distinguished by fancy decorations and exuberant color schemes. Architectural pattern books featured homes suitable for every lifestyle and pocketbook, with floor plans that incorporated multiple floors and rooms with specific purposes. The interest in verticality resulted in higher ceilings, and taller and larger windows than in earlier homes. Articles in newspapers and magazines on household taste and decorating styles featured illustrations of fashionable furniture, large-figured floral carpets, printed fabric, and wallpaper, as well as an assortment of bric-a-brac.

Early Victorian taste not only brought changes in style and technology to many households, but also dictated new preferences for factory-woven goods. Textiles of all varieties were now being produced by American industry—patterned cloth of wool, cotton, and silk, woven coverlets, lace, knitted goods, and patterned carpets. Virtually any type of thread or fabric was easily available from shopkeepers, dry goods establishments, and traveling peddlers. The Victorian consumer had a great love of complex and ornate designs, as well as a fascination with new technology and pride in its products, which found their way into elaborately furnished parlors and bedchambers.

Victorian Quiltmaking

Fashionable decorating trends influenced patterns, not only in factory-woven counterpanes, but also in all types of handmade bedcovers as well. Between the 1830s and 1860s, American quiltmakers created more pieced and appliqué quilts than ever before. Many factors contributed to this, including the increased availability of inexpensive fabric and an increased amount of leisure time created by better economic conditions. Books, periodicals, music, and other aspects of popular culture advocated and promoted needle arts as genteel, ladylike, and excellent moral pastimes for all women.

Periodicals included patterns and instructions, and the writings of other authors who encouraged the making of quilts. Hexagon patchwork, the first quilt pattern published in an American periodical, appeared in *Godey's Lady's Book* in January 1835. The author provided the pattern and instructions for making patchwork designs and also commented that "patchwork may be made in various forms,

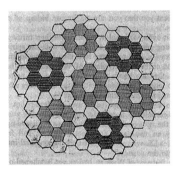

Hexagon pattern first published in *Godey's Lady's Book* in January 1835.

"The Quilting Party," *Godey's Lady's Book*, September 1849.

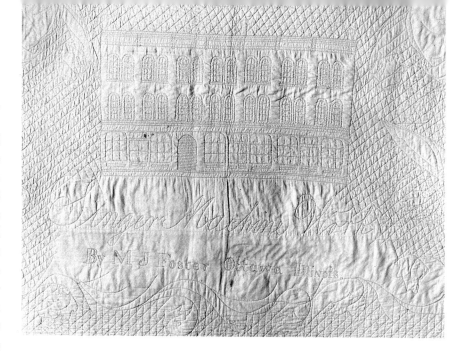

as stars, triangles, diamonds, waves, stripes, squares, etc."[45]

Authors of needlework columns and household advice books advised women to purchase new fabrics to make whole cloth quilts and intricately pieced and appliquéd quilts to brighten their bedchambers. One writer commented that ". . . quilts of old calico are seen only in inferior chambers . . ."[46] The continued and widespread interest in quiltmaking is also documented by numerous references in popular fiction and music. In September 1849 *Godey's Lady's Book* published the story "The Quilting Party" by T. S. Arthur and featured an illustration of a quilting bee.[47]

Needlework as a recreation was also promoted by various organizations and civic groups who sponsored exhibitions and fairs, featuring both industrially and domestically produced textiles and fancy work. First popular in the early decades of the 1800s, these fairs continue to operate today in rural areas around the country. Newspapers promoted these popular events and reported the prize winners. The Maryland Institute for the Promotion of Mechanics awarded several prizes at the 1850 exhibition; entries included a white counterpane made at Allendale Mills, Rhode Island; a Mathematical Star quilt, and a "fancy quilt" singled out as "worthy of notice" for its patriotic design.[48]

Detail. Whole Cloth Quilt, Central Medallion Pattern. 1850-1860. "Singer Machine Work." Made by M. J. Foster. Ottawa, Illinois. Cotton; machine-quilted. 83" x 82". Museum acquisition 1961-098. (10-405)
The invention of the sewing machine greatly reduced the time required to produce and maintain many household textiles and garments. Needlework, always highly prized as a skill, became increasingly an expression not only of creativity, but also of moral virtue expressed in the selfless dedication of hours of handiwork to beautify the home. Harriette Kidder acquired a sewing machine in 1859 to sew clothes for her five children. She found the new machine to be "a very valuable household article" and believed that "it render[ed] sewing a pleasure rather than a toil."[49]

"The New Sewing Machine,"
Godey's Lady's Book, March 1863.

The Emergence of Block Set Patterns in American Quilts

A distinctive development in quiltmaking in the mid-1800s is the emergence of block patterns—a term which refers to any arrangement of motifs either pieced or appliquéd, made in individual squares, then arranged and sewn together to make a whole quilt top. While this type of construction reached its fullest expression in the mid-nineteenth century, precursors for block style quilts can be seen in the pieced mosaic-style quilts made in England in the late eighteenth century and in the English and American quilts made of solid colored cloth quilted with blocks or diamonds set on point, each

page 58

block filled with a design.[50]

A number of factors might have led to the development and overwhelming popularity of block quilt designs in the mid-nineteenth century. One of the most likely sources of design inspiration is other textiles and furnishings made for the home, such as floor cloths, carpets, furnishing fabrics, wallpapers, and even floor tiles. Many of these items incorporated motifs 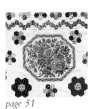 laid out in a grid of squares and framed or set off in a white space. Another example in the Shelburne Museum collection is a pieced quilt made by Jane Morton Cook whose design resembles a hexagon tile floor pattern with a central medallion set within a square and

page 51

framed with scattered hexagon designs. Floor cloths were often painted in direct imitation of tile and mosaic floors, patterns of interlocking squares and hexagons.[51] A piecework album quilt made by Mrs. Meacham in the 1840s incorporates a square tile-like pattern in its design.

Another source of inspiration for block patterned quilts would have been found in the newly available and widely popular jacquard-woven carpets and coverlets embellished with floral wreath and medallion patterns. These coverlets were typically woven with pattern motifs, which ranged in size from eight to fifteen inches, repeated in grid-like format, then framed with a floral or scenic border.

page 58

JACQUARD WEAVING

*T*he technology of weaving with a jacquard-pattern device was introduced to the American textile industry in the Philadelphia/New Jersey area sometime in the 1820s for the production of luxury brocade and damask silks in an effort to compete with French and English textile goods.

The jacquard attachment, which could be mounted on any large barn-frame loom, came at an opportune time for professional hand weavers, whose hand-woven goods had been superseded in the market place by inexpensive factory-woven cottons. Although its technological complexity, size, and cost made it unsuitable for home production, many professional weavers fit their looms with jacquard heads to produce carpets and coverlets patterned with elaborate floral and curvilinear patterns for the American market. The elaborately patterned coverlets could be designed with borders and corners which could include the name of the buyer, weaver, location, date, and even a motto. By the mid-1840s, homeowners, especially in the northeast, were very familiar with these fancy coverlets and, in all likelihood, if they themselves did not own one, they knew someone who did.[52]

Detail. Jacquard Coverlet, Floral Medallion Pattern. 1840-1841. Woven by Garret William Van Doren for Lucinda Housel Gary. Millstone, New Jersey. Cotton and wool. 85" x 83". Gift of Ruth Barnett 1989-40. (10-694)

Lucinda Housel was born in 1816, and died June 1900. She commissioned this coverlet in 1840.

Virtually every type of flower was recreated in cloth in the 1800s. Floral quilt patterns were inspired by a variety of sources, not the least of which was the rising interest in natural history, which also served as an inspiration for botanical patterns. By the mid-nineteenth century, parlors in most middle-class homes were likely to include a fern case, aquarium, shell cabinet, butterfly cabinet, or album of pressed flowers or seaweed. Suitable entertainment for the family might include a visit to a zoological garden or public garden, an evening of looking through the microscope, or a gathering walk to collect samples of shells, rocks, or plants.[53] The study of botany, especially by women, found its expression in painting, drawing, embroidery, and other forms of needlework, especially quiltmaking. This interest is documented by the seemingly endless array of floral patterns used in American quilts made from solid colored cloth. There was a fashion for quilts composed of floral sprays cut intact from glazed cotton chintz cloth and appliquéd to a plain ground, similar to the medallion quilts made earlier in the century. Victorians also enjoyed using various motifs, especially flowers, as symbols of emotion and sentiment. Some quilts featured a wide array of floral specimens, while others repeated a single stylized floral motif. Shelburne's quilt collection includes a wide variety of rose patterns as well as peony, coxcomb, lily, and tulip.

page 64

Floral quilt patterns also reflect the influence of rococo and classical revival styles. Flowers, fruits, and classical motifs found on furniture, decorative household accessories, and furnishing fabrics served as an inspiration for quiltmakers. This influence is most clearly seen in the elaborate wreaths, baskets, and urns which were used for appliqué quilts. This genre is epitomized by the album quilts made in Baltimore, Maryland, between the 1840s and 1850s. Made by expert needleworkers, they typically incorporate intricate layers of appliquéd motifs, the use of ombré printed fabrics, intricate quilting and embroidery techniques, and a variety of complex, highly pictorial designs. Many of the realistic floral and fruit patterns relate to the carved motifs which decorate the furniture made popular by John Belter. Of the five Baltimore-style album quilts in

page 55

Shelburne's collection, the most elaborate features floral hearts, baskets, and wreaths, as well as a memorial commemorating Mexican War hero Samuel Ringgold, and two patriotic eagles made of ombré fabric.[54]

Many geometric quilt patterns probably found their inspiration in one of the design books published in the 1800s. In 1856 Owen Jones published a design book entitled *The Grammar of Ornament* which presented the arts and decorative motifs of other cultures as a source of design. The author included 112 color-plate illustrations from such exotic places as Greece, Rome, Japan, and China. In Jones's examples of Roman tile patterns, a person familiar with nineteenth-century needlework can recognize the source of such nineteenth-century quilt patterns as Flying Geese, Nine Patch, and Stars.

page 61

One type of quilt mirrors a popular mid-nineteenth-century activity, the custom of assembling a journal or album with signatures of friends and relatives, verses, and

Paint decorated stand, New England, 1830-1840. Workstands made by young women at seminaries typically were decorated with floral motifs.

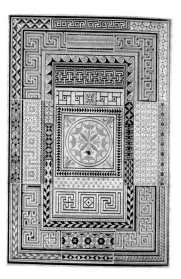

Tile patterns *Pompeii #3*. Owen Jones (1809-1874), an English architect and art decorator, was the Superintendent of Works for the 1851 London Exhibition and was in charge of decorating the Crystal Palace in London. His work inspired both William Morris and the Arts and Crafts Movement.[55]

Flower Basket and Nine-Patch Pattern Quilt. 1850-1860. Maker unknown. Northeastern United States. Cotton, whole cloth. 93" x 89". Gift of Electra H. Webb 1957-652. (10-262) Faux-quilt fabric, made by both American and English textile printers, was often used to make whole cloth quilts. This quilt is filled with combed cotton and backed with tan, floral printed ombré and a printed check cotton.

drawings. A friendship album quilt is the cloth version of the autograph album, both intended as a treasured token and reminder of friends. Pieced and/or appliquéd quilt blocks were made by either one quilter or a group of friends, autographed, then assembled in a bedcover. Finished quilts were often made as gifts to commemorate and mark an important occasion, a parting, or a passage in life.[56] Album quilts in the Shelburne collection exhibit the variety of designs incorporated in this style of bedcover. In some quilts, the pattern blocks were made of the same pieced or appliquéd patterns. In others, a quilt block maker selected a pattern of her choice to be included in the quilt. The quilt blocks would then be carefully inscribed or stamped with a name. Another type of album quilt in the Shelburne collection descended through the Mitchell family of eastern Pennsylvania. Typical of a style used by many Quakers of the Philadelphia and northern New Jersey area, it is made in a geometric pieced pattern, sometimes called sawtooth triangles, with the alternating white triangles inscribed with a signature, biblical passage, poem or inked drawing.[57]

page 56

Heavily stuffed and tied whole cloth quilts, often called comforters or "comfortables," continued to be popular throughout the nineteenth century. Miss Leslie described them in *The House Book* as "soft thick quilts, used as substitutes for blankets, and laid under the bedspread. One of them is equal in warmth to three heavy blankets; and they are excellent in cold winters for persons who like to sleep extremely warm." She went on to describe, ". . . a comfortable for a large or double bed ought to be three yards long and three yards wide. You may

page 59

make it of glazed colored muslin (in which case it cannot be washed) or of furniture chintz, or cheap calico. . . . the above size will require 3 pounds of carded cotton bats. It should be quilted in very large diamonds."[58]

While hand weavers, quilters, and other needleworkers were following styles set by the carpet, fabric, and wallpaper industry, textile manufacturers were in turn influenced by the popularity of quilts. As early as the 1850s fabric printing companies produced cotton yard goods, called "faux quilts," printed with piecework quilt patterns. Quilters incorporated these innovative patterns in making whole cloth quilts. Shelburne's collection contains examples of four different patterns: a Nine Patch with Flower Baskets, a central medallion pieced star, a hexagon with sprays of blooming lilacs, and a Log Cabin.

White bedchambers and bedcovers, popular in the late eighteenth century, enjoyed a resurgence in the mid-nineteenth century. Easily washed white curtains and bedcovers appealed to the Victorian housewife's concern for hygiene as they "always contrived to have a clean appearance."[59] The fashion for white was encouraged by a number of factors, not the least of which were the increasing availability of factory-woven white cotton fabric and improving technology for washing clothes. White-work quilts and embroidered bedcovers with large central designs embellished with twined and scrolled feathers, flowers, architectural, and figural motifs became fashionable in the northern states. The use of a central medallion pattern coincides with the popularity of large figured carpets and jacquard-woven bedspreads made in the mid-nineteenth century.

page 57

At this same time, mock-Marseilles quilts appeared on the market. The name is derived from the hand-woven quilts of the same name, originally made in Marseilles, France, in the eighteenth century. Nineteenth-century mill owners eager to capitalize on the popular interest for heavily stuffed white-work quilts adapted power looms to weave affordable copies of handmade examples. Factory-woven Marseilles quilts were made entirely on a power loom with all three quilt layers—top, back, and filler—woven simultaneously.[60] The continued popularity of embroidered covers is illustrated by counterpanes of white cloth embroidered with white yarn and candlewick that incorporate the central medallions and wreaths, mimicking designs seen in both Marseilles and hand-sewn quilts.

The Late Nineteenth-Century and Post-Civil War America

The Civil War disrupted the making of quilts for the beautification of the home. Women had little time for fancy work; their sewing skills were dedicated to providing clothing and warm quilts for their troops. For several years the production of American cotton cloth was disrupted by the focus on military needs and lack of raw material; the importing of cloth from Europe was hampered by military activity in coastal ports. Women were apt to recut and reuse existing garments for clothing rather than purchase new goods. Utilitarian and special occasion quilts were also likely to be made of reused goods.

In the years following the Civil War, people refocused on domestic activities in their desire to return to pre-war normalcy and stability, and quiltmaking once again became a popular pastime. Factories were able to return to the production of domestic goods, safe shipping routes were reestablished, and men home from the war returned to work, all of which contributed to a resurgence in the economy. By the 1870s, however, it was clear that the pervasive nature of industrialization had irrevocably changed the face of the nation's towns and cities as well as the attitudes of its people. The increased mechanization resulted in a lack of personal involvement by the individual worker, and ultimately a loss of craftsmanship. At the same time, increased competition in the marketplace caused the production of lower quality goods. Americans became increasingly aware of the contradiction between pride in the industrial and economic progress, and nostalgia for the simpler lifestyle of an earlier era. This duality provided the context for the next generation of quilters.

Interiors of the post-Civil War era were characterized by a combination of many colors, textures, and patterns. The creation of a fashionable room required many different types of textiles for upholstery, bedcovers, carpets, and window and door curtains. Fortunately, the American textile industry was able to provide large amounts of inexpensive and readily available cloth. Between the years 1860 and 1900, the American textile industry experienced unprecedented growth. Companies throughout the northeast produced millions of yards of fabric each year—a wide variety of printed, checked, and plaid cotton and wool. Textile producers sought ways to maximize cloth production and minimize costs. New machinery was developed in an effort to mechanize all aspects of cloth production, and many hand-controlled techniques were eliminated. Factory-wide standardization resulted in the mass production of all types of cloth. New technology for printing cloth had increased the numbers of colors which could be printed in one run from five or

NO. 4.
Patented February 20th, 1872.

	PER DOZ.
Tapestry	$35.00
Brussels	37.00
Velvet	42.00
For making, customers' own Carpet, net,	24.00

No. 4, Twelve Yards Carpet, per doz.

American Ottoman and Hassock Company advertisement. The Slipperbox ottoman incorporates design motifs made popular by William Morris.[61]

six to as many as fourteen. Floral prints  continued to be popular. Paisley patterns and printed weaves were also fashionable. Cloth was printed to mimic more

page 101

expensive woven goods which were ribbed, watered, or woven in small-figured dobby patterns or damask with two closely related shades of colors.

In 1861 William Morris and John Ruskin founded the Aesthetic Movement, an English decorating style, which emphasized the necessity of integrating art and function into good design. Their designs were introduced to Americans at the Centennial Exhibition in 1876, and by 1881 they had attracted an international following. Proponents of the Aesthetic Movement adapted decorative and exotic motifs and patterns traditionally used in such countries as China, India, and Japan into wallpaper, ceramics, carpets, textiles, and other decorative arts for the English and American markets.

In June 1865 Charles L. Eastlake published the first in a series of articles entitled *Hints on Household Taste*, in which he hoped to "improve taste in objects of modern manufacture" and "encourage a discrimination between good and bad design . . . ."[63] The series, which outlined what came to be known as the Eastlake style, was so popular that the articles were republished as a book in 1868. The first American edition, published in 1872, enjoyed considerable success, and seven editions were subsequently printed. Eastlake, a scholar of the English Middle Ages, artist, and proponent of the Gothic Revival, advised homeowners to avoid the mid-Victorian taste, which he felt "was based on eclecticism rather than tradition," and consequently was "capricious and subject to constant variation."[64] Like many designers of his time, he deplored the loss of craftsmanship caused by an increased reliance on mechanized tools. "It is the spirit and principles of early

Drawing-Room Sofa, executed by Jackson & Graham from a design by Charles L. Eastlake, from his book, *Hints on Household Taste*.[62]

manufacture which I desire to see revived," he stated, "not the absolute forms." Eastlake's philosophy reflects the ideas that motivated the handicraft revival and Arts and Crafts Movements. He stressed simplicity of line and form, incorporated little ornamentation in his designs, and believed that furniture should be functional. The style, sometimes called "modern Gothic," inspired furniture, textiles, and paper which emphasized vertical lines, geometric shapes, surfaces divided by decorative banding, and the use of incised lines for stylized ornamentation.

In the late 1880s, ladies' magazines often included columns and articles on home decorating, offering advice on fashionable color schemes and appropriate fabrics. Writers considered cotton prints acceptable as fashionable furnishing fabrics as long as they were used in a fitting manner in informal situations. In general, the bedroom was deemed the most appropriate place for cotton prints. Developments in the dyestuff industry between 1856 and 1880, however, made new colors available for lightweight wools as well as cottons, including magenta, blue, orange, red, green, yellow, and black. Wool cloth printed in these new colors was popular for both clothing and furnishing fabric, as it had the same bright colors as silk, but was less expensive.

Several cotton print manufactories of this era featured furnishing fabrics with bucolic scenes of country life, which presented an idealized view of life before railroads, steam power, and modern urban life—floral landscapes with children at play, hunting scenes with men and hounds, and couples playing tennis. *The Curtainmaker's Handbook* published in 1889 advised that cretonnes, like chintz, gave "a fresh and charming home-feeling to the apartment." Cretonne was first publicized by Eastlake in 1868 as a colorful, serviceable cloth for bed furniture and "a good substitute for chintz, in so far as it will wash, and does not depend for effect on a high glaze." In 1879 Mrs. H. W. Beecher commented on the "softness of the cloth [and] the delicacy of colour" which made it one of the "most desir-

page 69

able and attractive materials for furnishing a country, or summer home."[65] Many quiltmakers used the gaily printed cottons for whole cloth quilts.

Meanwhile, increased mechanization in the weaving industry produced looms capable of weaving cloth in complex patterns and with multiple colors—silk damasks, brocades, and even embroideries. Jacquard looms were also now steampowered, thereby reducing the cost of figured carpeting and bedcovers. By 1900 American textile manufacturing companies were producing as much silk dress fabric as was being imported from around the world. Recognizing the popularity of quiltmaking and realizing the potential market, silk companies packaged remnants  of satin, brocade, velvet, and other richly woven fabrics for use in quilts. Quiltmakers took advantage of the lustrous texture, elegant patterns, and vibrant colors of the available silk fabric to transform traditional patterns into

page 77

Hall Trees, Mirrors, and Mantels. *Rockford Furniture Journal*, August 15, 1890.[67]

virtual kaleidoscopes of pattern and color.

In the last quarter of the nineteenth century, magazine articles urged American women to furnish their homes with American-made textiles. Authors advised women, especially those who did not work outside the home, to decorate their homes with their own fancy needlework. During this era, hand-sewn quilts, and knit and crocheted bedcovers, which along with the bedstead had been banished from the parlor to the bedchamber in the early 1800s, now returned to the parlor, where they once again reflected status, Victorian taste, and women's "civilizing" influence.[66]

Popular Trends in Quiltmaking

A growing interest in international events and industrial expansion in the last quarter of the nineteenth century led the American and European communities and many industrial leaders to promote international expositions which featured new technology and products from different nations. The Centennial Exposition in Philadelphia in 1876 hosted nations from around the world. Each country sponsored an exhibit pavilion which displayed its products and advances in technology as well as its way of life, history, culture, arts, and crafts. Nearly ten million Americans visited the Exposition, an event which now can be seen to have had a tremendous influence on

page 62

Numerous letters and diaries contain references to these log cabins. While traveling by train from Milton, Wisconsin, to her new home in Burke, Ellen Reed saw many log homes—some with no doors or windows, only blankets or quilts to keep out animals and strangers. She and her husband Willard planned to build a log cabin before a wood-framed house could be constructed.[68]

subsequent art and culture in America.

Publicity about Japanese and Chinese exhibits at the Centennial Exposition and a current fashion for decorating in the Aesthetic style resulted in an enthusiasm for nearly everything which reflected Asian taste and design. In quiltmaking this led to the introduction and subsequent popularity of a new quiltmaking technique called "crazy" patchwork. Pattern blocks were made by sewing irregular shaped pieces together in random fashion, then embellishing them with embroidery, woven and printed ribbons, and/or hand-painted scenes. Embroidery patterns used along the seams often mimicked incised decoration on Eastlake furniture and architecture.

By 1887, however, magazines were announcing the end of this quilting trend. One author "regretted much of the time and energy spent on the most childish and unsatisfactory of all work done with the needle, 'crazy' patchwork."[69] Despite the change in fashion, women continued to make crazy quilts

page 70

through the early twentieth century, incorporating available cotton, silk, and later, rayon goods.

The era of industrialization was exciting for some, but for many it

page 66

provoked a sense of nostalgia for craftsmanship, simpler times, a sense of home, and rural lifestyles. Exhibits of early American tools, furniture, and textiles of early settlement days at the Centennial Exposition celebrated the anniversary of the nation's birth and served as a reminder of the past. During this time many people

page 63

began the systematic collecting of American relics, items of history which illustrated a style of life that was quickly passing by. Some people

expressed this by preserving early quilts, coverlets, and decorative bedcovers, others by reviving traditional hand-weaving and needlework traditions, especially cotton patchwork.

Throughout the late nineteenth and twentieth centuries, the popularity of traditional cotton patchwork patterns persisted. Patterns for appliqué and piecework designs, now distributed nationally, became less expensive

page 60

and more available to the average consumer. Household and ladies' magazines

page 71

such as *Peterson's, Good Housekeeping,* and *The American Agriculturist* published new patterns. In 1889 the Ladies' Art Company sold pieced and appliqué quilt patterns and sample books through the mail. They published the first known brochure of quilt patterns in 1898, titled *Diagrams of Quilt Sofa and Pin Cushion Patterns.* Within thirty years the company published and distributed over five hundred quilt designs.[70]

page 66

Quilt patterns are often inspired by popular culture. The Log Cabin pattern was introduced in the late nineteenth century. Quilt scholar Rod Kiracofe refers to it as "one of the most American of all quilt designs."[71] The log cabin was a symbol of America's expansion west as territories were opened for settlement: Texas in 1845, Oregon in 1846, and California in 1848, to name a few. Thousands of people left their homes in the east to carve out a homestead. Typically their first dwelling was either a log or sod house.

The use of the log cabin image as a political campaign symbol is also thought to have been an inspiration for the quilt pattern. William Harrison used the log cabin in his 1840 presidential campaign, and it appeared as a decorative motif in at least two roller-print cotton textiles.[72] Abraham Lincoln also used the log cabin motif in his early political campaigns. The earliest documented Log Cabin quilt is dated 1869, and more are known to have been made in the 1870s.[73] Its resurgence in the late 1880s and 1890s is probably related to Benjamin Harrison's Log Cabin presidential campaign of 1888, which inspired a variety of political memorabilia in the shape of log cabins.

The popularity of the Log Cabin pattern is documented by the numerous quilts made in silk, cotton, and wool fabrics in patterns as varied as Courthouse Steps, Windmill Blades,

page 69

Barn Raising, and Straight Furrow. Throughout the twentieth century, quiltmakers have used these patterns to pro-

page 68

duce bed quilts in full, crib, and doll sizes, as well as other household accessories including chair seats, pillows, and pot holders. Log Cabin quilt patterns typically contrast areas of light and dark cloth to dramatically emphasize the geometric pattern.

In the late 1800s, there was a public fascination for quilts made from thousands of tiny pieces of fabric. Newspapers sponsored quilt contests, offering prizes to the person who could make a quilt with the highest number of pieces. An article published in the *St. Louis Post-Dispatch* related the story about Mrs. Walter Zoll of Poplar Bluff, Missouri, who made a quilt which contained twenty-one thousand, eight-hundred forty pieces. Reading the newspaper account of Mrs. Zoll's project sparked the competitive spirit in a Mrs. Long and inspired her to piece a quilt "containing thirty-eight thousand pieces. She sewed it entirely by hand, using twenty spools of

thread," and completed it five months later, on her seventy-eighth birthday.[74] Quilts made in this genre often incorporate squares or triangles of various patterns and colors, as the achievement of an overall

page 67

pattern was less important than the quantity of pieces. Some quiltmakers, however, managed to combine both objectives in their quilt project. Clarissa Alford made a quilt in the Windmill Blades pattern which incorporated more than six thousand pieces.

An unknown quilter from Ballston Spa, New York, used half-inch squares in a mosaic technique to produce a quilt featuring motifs as varied as an African American figure, cross on the mount, lock, chalice, and dog. The use of tiny half-inch pieces of fabric in building the design might have been inspired by the Postage Stamp quilts popular in the late 1800s. The use of motifs arranged on a grid format indicates that the quiltmaker developed the pattern after embroidery and needlework patterns popular at the time. Similar images were published in magazines and workbooks designed for woolen

Sawyer's Cabin, Shelburne Museum. From East Charlotte, Vermont, 1800.

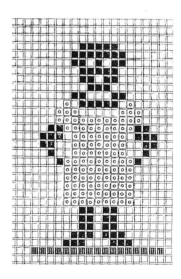

Embroidery and Worsted Cross-stitch Patterns, J. F. Ingalls, Lynn, Massachusetts. (Collection of Merikay Waldvogel; Photo: Doug Smiley)

embroidery, Berlin work, pulled thread embroidery, and darned net work. In fact, the pattern for the African American figure appears in an 1870s pattern book entitled *Embroidery and Worsted Cross-Stitch Patterns*.[75] The dog, cross, and lyre motifs identical to those used in the Ballston Spa quilt also appear on an embroidered sampler in the collection of the Abby Aldrich Rockefeller Folk Art Center.[76] The relationship between the embroidered and patchwork motifs is unmistakable and provides a fascinating connection between popular needlework traditions and trends.

page 72

The New Century

*I*n the first decades of the twentieth century, new inventions, new products, and new means of transportation transformed the lives of most Americans. The advent of electricity brought such modern conveniences as washing machines, flatirons, vacuum cleaners, and central heating. Fewer people needed to quilt for necessity, but the popular appeal of quilts continued to reach new audiences.[77]

The style of interior decoration now called "Colonial Revival," which originated in the centennial year, turned to the American past as a source of inspiration for the modern home. Advocates of the Colonial Revival style believed that art, architecture, and furnishings made before 1840—when America entered the industrial age—possessed "integrity of workmanship, thoughtful use of honest, sound materials, and accurate awareness of design principles."[78] This style rejected the previous decorating modes as ostentatious and cluttered; the new Colonial style was seen as simple, clean, and restful. Contemporary home and decorating magazines featured articles on how to evoke the spirit of the Colonial past by decorating rooms with American antiques, combined with contemporary wallpaper, fabric, and furnishings adapted from American forms dating from early settlement to 1840. Quilts complemented this new style of decorating and were frequently featured in magazines. The editors of *The Modern Priscilla* noted, "Every woman who is fortunate enough to possess one of the patchwork quilts of the ante-bellum period is displaying it proudly as part of her guest bedroom equipment."[79]

Historians and antiquarians of this time placed a high value on the tangible accomplishments of their ancestors. Quilts were cherished by descendants of the quiltmaker, and valued for the quality of the work, the skill of the maker, and the memory of the ancestor. They were passed lovingly from family member to family member. The next owner was often selected by measuring their appreciation for the cherished heirloom textile and their ability to care for it. Lots were sometimes drawn to choose the future owner, especially when more than one person in the family wanted a quilt. A quilt in Shelburne's collection known as *Sunburst and Sawtooth* was passed through the family in this way. An envelope attached to the quilt and marked: "Fannie's Sunburst and Sawtooth Quilt" contained this note: "This Sunburst and Sawtooth Quilt was pieced by Eunice Baker, my grandfather's sister who was born in Pawlet, Vermont. It was given to John and Mary Miller Baker by her daughter Mary Euling

page 64

Baldwin and was drawn by lot by Fannie Baker May 7th, 1908. M.E.B."

Exhibitions of American furniture and quilts at major American museums and galleries combined with the Colonial Revival style to develop a popular interest in decorating with American antique furniture, household accessories, and textiles —especially quilts. Private individuals and museums began to assemble quilt collections, dealers bought and sold antique quilts, and publishers issued books about making, collecting, and using quilts in the home. Author Carrie Hall commented in *The Romance of the Patchwork Quilt in America*, published in 1935, that "without money for costly diversions, the women have turned to a renewal of quiltmaking. . . . the making of quilts in the home has become astonishingly popular."[80]

As the popularity of making cotton patchwork quilts grew, more and more patterns became available. Quilt designs were published in books, pamphlets, and home and decorating magazines. Even local newspapers offered columns on quiltmaking. Carrie Hall and Rose Kretsinger documented hundreds of traditional quilt designs in their 1935 book *The Romance of the Patchwork Quilt in America*.[81] Lockport Batting Company and the Rock River Cotton Company offered free patterns inside their rolls of batting. Stearns & Foster published such pattern booklets as the *Mountain Mist Blue Book of Famous Quilt Patterns* in 1935.

Vera Bryant Woodward of Ohio was clearly inspired by the Colonial Revival to produce five quilts for her home, two traditional patterns and three others which

incorporated more contemporary motifs and color schemes—an Irish Chain pattern in blue and white, Drunkard's Path in red and white, and Currant and Coxcomb, Flowering Hearts, and Double Hearts and Birds.

Brochure cover advertising quilt kits. c. 1930.

Fabric manufacturers capitalized on the Colonial Revival style by featuring cotton prints reminiscent of mid- to late nineteenth-century fabrics, small sprigged floral and large flowered chintz in all-over and striped prints. They also researched and reproduced many small floral prints which had been popular in early years. These patterns were suitable for clothing, furnishing, and quiltmaking. Many quiltmakers and artists designed and made quilts which they hoped would recapture the charm of nineteenth-century textiles.

Florence Cowdin Peto was an accomplished quiltmaker who enjoyed combining new fabrics with scraps of antique cloth in her quilts. She first collected and researched quilts as a hobby, but her interest in historical quilting traditions and techniques led her to develop this interest as a professional pursuit. In 1939 Peto wrote to Emma Andres, "My photographs of American-made quilts, spreads, and woven coverlets number over three hundred—all have authentic histories verified by family records and papers. . . . What I desire to do in gathering this material [is to] preserve the memory and identity of the quiltmaker as well as her needlework."[82] Peto

Fabric scraps from Florence Peto's collection. Gift of Joyce Gross.

influenced thousands of quilters and quilt collectors in her career which included lecturing, writing articles for such magazines as *American Home* and *Woman's Day*, and publishing two books, *American Quilts and Coverlets* and *Historic Quilts*.

One of the major innovations in quilt-making was the trend of designers creating new quilt patterns. Marie Webster, the needlework editor for *Ladies Home Journal* from 1911 to 1917, operated a quilt pattern business from her home in Marion, Indiana. Other designers who designed, published, and sold quilt patterns included Carlie Sexton Holmes, a contributor to *Better Homes and Gardens*, and Ann Champe Orr, art and needlework editor for *Good Housekeeping* from 1919 to 1940. The quilt designs created by these talented women reflected the influence of the decorative aesthetic of the time, the use of soft, pastel colors, an emphasis on clean uncluttered lines, and the combination of popular decorative motifs in a traditional format. The designs were advertised in magazines and were sold as kits and published patterns.

Olga Six Baker made a quilt with Marie Webster's Wind-Blown Tulip pattern in the 1930s while she was teaching school in Chicago. The pattern, first featured in the *Ladies Home Journal* in January 1911, was included in Webster's 1915 book,

page 73

Quilts: Their Story and How to Make Them with the caption, "Seems to bring a breath of spring-time both in form and color. Even the border flowers seem to be waving and nodding in the breeze." [83]

While quilts continued to be appreciated as bed coverings, heirlooms, and historical documents, the major innovation for the quilt world in the twentieth century was a new appreciation of quilts as art. A quilt in the Museum's collection, entitled "Under his Wings," illustrates this concept. Bertha Amelia Meckstroth (1875-1960) of Glencoe, Illinois, who was trained as a sculptress, gave up marble to create quilts, which she called "Sculptures in Cloth." [84] She heavily stuffed her figures and designs to give a sculptured, three-dimensional feeling to her quilts and used reverse appliqué for the calligraphic script. Meckstroth designed and sewed the quilt top, but hired a seamstress to quilt the layers together, a step she considered tedious. An exhibition of her quilts

page 13

entitled, "Sculpture and Paintings in Cotton, Linen and Silk" was featured at the 1933 Century of Progress Exposition. The catalogue described her work: "Her medium of expression is cotton, linen, and silk which she combines with skilled needlework, with novel effects in color and with dimensional depth, until it becomes a painting, a statue, or a tiny figure molded in fabric." [85]

Throughout the history of quiltmaking in America, women have found ways to combine artistic concerns with utilitarian needs. Quilts and bedcovers, once designed for warmth and privacy, continue to be important elements of decoration in the home and often serve as both personal and public expressions of creativity. Similarly, current day quiltmakers, like their predecessors in the 1700s and 1800s, incorporate elements of traditional design with the widest possible range of available fabrics to expand the horizons of this textile art. Collections of heirloom quilts like those at the Shelburne Museum are important as a resource for the quilters of today and as a part of the enduring legacy that will be passed on to the quilters of tomorrow.

GALLERY:
Quilts from the
Shelburne Museum

**Pieced Quilt, Tide Mill Pattern. 1785-1810.
Made by Mary Dingee Priestley (1767-1849).
Ossining, New York. Cotton and linen. Marked
"M.P." on the back in cross-stitch. 97" x 91".
Museum acquisition 1964-43. (10-448)**

Mary Dingee was born in 1767 near Ossining, New
York. Family tradition relates that Mary pieced this
quilt using fabric cut from her own trousseau
clothes purchased in Philadelphia, as well as clothing belonging to her family.[1]

This quilt was purchased from the maker's
great-niece by Ruth Finley, quilt collector and
author of the 1929 book *Old Patchwork Quilts and
the Women Who Made Them*. It was later acquired
by Electra Webb for the Museum collection.

**Appliquéd Counterpane, Cornucopia
Medallion Pattern. 1800-1825. Maker
unknown. New England, northeastern
United States. Cotton. 100" x 100". Gift of
Electra H. Webb 1952-552. (10-029)**

This appliqué incorporates two of the most popular neoclassical designs, an urn with flowers and a
cornucopia. The cornucopia, or horn of plenty,
filled with flowers is inspired by the Greek legend
of Jupiter, who endowed it with the magic power
of becoming filled with whatever its owner wished.

Appliquéd and Pieced Counterpane, Floral Medallion Pattern. 1814. Made by Ann Robinson. New England, possibly Connecticut. Cotton; marked "Ann Robinson October 1, 1813" and "Finished January 27, 1814." 100" x 95". Museum acquisition 1954-439. (10-140)

This floral medallion quilt made by Ann Robinson illustrates the influence of classical design on American quiltmaking. The neoclassical style of decorating swept America in the late eighteenth century. Incorporating Greek architectural forms and decorative elements into American architecture, clothing, furniture design, wallpaper, textiles, and needlework seemed the perfect way to express the ideals of the new democracy. Popular motifs included wreaths of flowers, urns, garlands, lyres, acanthus leaves, and shields. Ann Robinson demonstrated her knowledge of classical design when she used a large laurel wreath to frame the center diamond medallion and a smaller wreath to frame her cross-stitched signature.

**Pieced and Appliquéd Quilt, Medallion with
Diamond and Sawtooth Border. 1810-1820.
Attributed to Mrs. Vigors. London, England.
Cotton. 96 ¹/₂" x 104". Museum acquisition
1958-211. (10-304)**

The popularity of the central medallion design
framed by pieced bands is illustrated by this
English quilt. The pieces of chintz and other printed

cottons are sewn over paper reinforcements.
Some of the papers are from letters addressed to
Mrs. Vigors in Marylebone postmarked 1808.
The maker also used part of a lottery ticket,
"No. 15222," announcing the grand prize of
40,000 pounds held by the Branscomb offices on
Holborn and Cornhill Streets, Haymarket. The stub
also mentions lotteries held in 1806 and 1807.

Appliquéd Quilt Top, Octagon Pattern with Figures. 1782-1800. Made by an ancestor of the Spaulding family. Townsend, Massachusetts. Cotton and linen copperplate printed on a brown and white cotton ground. 78" x 98". Museum acquisition 1957-533. (10-242)

Textile printers often copied images from contemporary English drawings and engravings. The cock and hen image was taken from Plate 79 of the *Ladies Amusement*, drawn by C. Fenn and engraved by P. Benazech. The scenes "Playing at Marbles" and "Spinning Top" were published in 1787 and 1788 by Bartolozzi after works by William Hamilton.[2] The copperplate toile fabrics of naval and military scenes

commemorate England's victory in 1782 when Commander Elliot seized Gibraltar from Spain.

This quilt descended through the family of Governor Roland Harty Spaulding (b.1873) of Rochester, New Hampshire. It was made either by Governor Spaulding's great-grandmother Sibyl Spaulding, or by his grandmother Lydia Cadwick Noell Spaulding.

Right: Governor Roland Harty Spaulding

Block-Printed and Painted Palampore, Floral and Bird Medallion Pattern. 1780-1820. Maker unknown. India. Cotton. 102" x 115 1/2". Gift of Electra H. Webb 1952-615. (10-095)
Motifs printed on this palampore relate to patterns used in American quilts, including serpentine vine, urn with flowers, and floral vine borders.

Appliquéd and Embroidered Counterpane, Floral Bouquet and Bird Medallion Pattern. 1800-1830. Maker unknown. Found in Reynoldsburg, Ohio. Linen, cotton, and wool yarns. 94" x 93". Museum acquisition 1958-060. (10-278)
This counterpane features floral and bird motifs cut from block-printed fabric appliquéd in repeating borders around an embroidered central medallion. The embroidery techniques used include satin stitch, chain stitch, buttonhole stitch, and French knots.

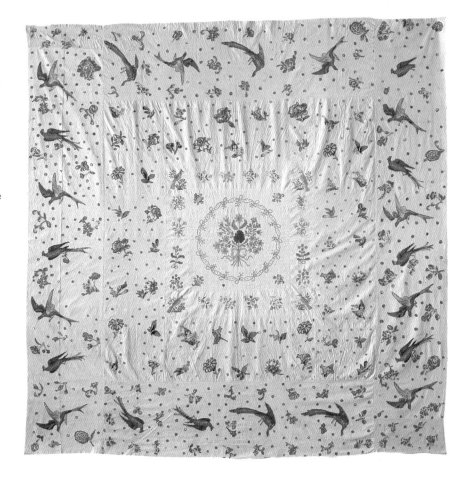

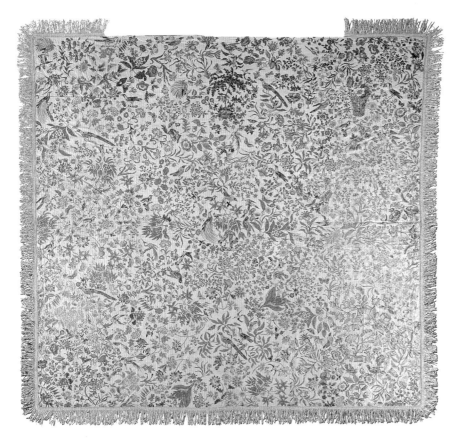

Appliquéd Quilt, All-over Floral Pattern. 1800-1820. Maker unknown. Northeastern United States. Cotton prints, linen ground, hand-spun and hand-woven linen fringe. 92³/₄" x 98". Gift of Mrs. Giles Whiting 1959-238. (10-361)

Quilts with small floral and bird motifs scattered randomly across a plain cloth ground are surely adapted from the patterns seen in printed palampores and woven carpets. The fringe is hand-woven of two-ply hand-spun linen thread.

Printed Palampore Counterpane, Floral Pattern. 1790-1820. Owned by Betsy A. Fuller. New England. Cotton. 116" x 103". Gift of Mrs. Harold Conner 1956-646. (10-311)

Seashells were a popular motif in neoclassical design. The popularity of gathering seashells began in the late eighteenth century, promoted by various publications on natural history.

**Whole Cloth Quilt, Serpentine Vine Print.
1774-1800. Made by a member of the
Roland family. New Holland, Pennsylvania.
Cotton. 92" x 98 ¹/₂". Museum acquisition
1958. (10-319)**

The fabric used to make this quilt was printed at
Bromley Hall, Manchester, England, sometime after
1774. A pattern book from the print works, now
in the collection of the Victoria and Albert
Museum in London, documents the origins of this
fabric. Only three examples of this textile have
survived: the first is this example maintained here
at the Shelburne Museum, the second is in the
Metropolitan Museum of Art in New York, and the
third is in the d'Allemage Collection in Paris.

The quilt, which shows little wear, was brought
into the Kinzer family of New Holland when a
descendant of the maker married a Kinzer in the
mid-1800s. Another quilt in the Shelburne collection, a variation of the Caesar's Crown pattern,
was made by Miss Elizabeth C. Kinzer.

**Pieced Quilt, Stripe Pattern. 1800-1820.
Made by a member of the Brush family.
Cambridge, Vermont. Glazed worsted wool.
98" x 95". Museum acquisition 1991-056.
(10-714)**

The small town of Cambridge, in north central
Vermont, was settled in 1783 by John Spafford.
According to a history of the town, he cleared
two acres of land, planted corn, and built a log
house covered with bark before going home to
Pierpoint, New Hampshire, to bring back his wife
and two children. Reportedly, "... the cabin was
small, with no windows, and a bed quilt was used
for a door the first winter." Another early settler
of Cambridge was Abner Brush (1763-1831), who
came from Long Island with his wife, Ruth. A tailor
by trade, Brush also operated an inn for many years
and served as the postmaster of Cambridge.[3]

By the early 1800s, a number of families named
Brush lived in the Cambridge area, including the
households of Abner, Jonathan, John, and Nathaniel
Brush. Further research might help us determine
which of the Brush women made this striped quilt.

Pieced Quilt, Hexagon Medallion. 1820-1840. Made by Jane Morton Cook. Scituate or Ipswich, Massachusetts. Cotton. 115" x 99". Museum acquisition 1957-524. (10-240)

Jane Morton Cook was born in Scituate, Massachusetts, the daughter of Caleb and Esther Morton Cook. While numerous Cook families lived in the Plymouth County-Scituate area, preliminary research has not uncovered information of either Caleb, Esther, or Jane Cook.

The hexagon pattern was used extensively in England from the late eighteenth through the nineteenth century. Another hexagon pattern quilt in the Museum collection, made in 1835 by E.A. Norris, incorporates a textile which commemorates King William IV, who was known as the Sailor King of England.

Appliquéd and Embroidered Counterpane, Tree of Life in Scalloped Medallion. 1820-1840. Maker unknown. North or South Carolina. Cotton. 106" x 98". Museum acquisition 1957. (10-236)

This neoclassical quilt is very similar in overall design to quilts made in Tidewater, Virginia, and North and South Carolina. The scalloped medallion was especially popular with southern quiltmakers.

Pieced Quilt, Four Patch and Nine Patch Pattern. 1820-1840. Owned by Harriet E. Brock. Newbury, Vermont. Cotton. 80" x 67". Gift of Mrs. Leonard N. Brock 1955-528. (10-148)

Harriet E. Brock, born in 1818, was the daughter of Jacob and Abigail Brock of South Newbury, Vermont. In his younger years Jacob Brock (b.1785) worked as a raftsman guiding huge rafts of logs down river, but after his marriage built a house and settled into farming. He was married four times. His first wife, Abigail Sanders, had twelve children; his second, Betsy Sinclair (d.1849), had three. He married his third wife, Abigail Eastman, in 1850, and his fourth wife, Mehetable Kimball Tice, in 1856.

The quilt remained in the Brock family until it was given to the Museum in 1955. A calling card engraved "Harriet E. Brock" was attached to the quilt with this note: "Over 100 years old / all sewed over & over. Some / of the small squares pieced / 4 times showing how much / print was valued".

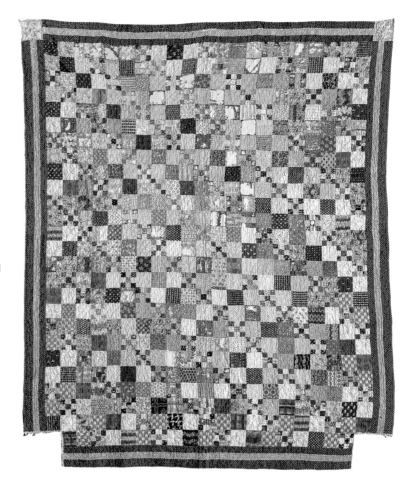

**Appliquéd Quilt, Rose and Bud Pattern.
1840-1860. Maker unknown. Northeastern
United States. Cotton. 96" x 78". Gift of
Electra H. Webb 1952-541. (10-018)**
Electra Webb acquired this quilt for her personal
collection, probably attracted to it by the use of
elaborately quilted and stuffed flower baskets and
sprays. The numerous quilts made with rose patterns illustrate the popularity of this flower in the
mid-nineteenth century. Victorians enjoyed using
different flowers as symbols to express an emotion. The rose, for instance, symbolized love.

**Whole Cloth Stenciled Quilt, Oak Leaf &
Orange Slice Pattern. 1840-1850. Maker
unknown. Attributed to New York. Cotton.
89" x 83 ¹/₄". Museum acquisition 1959-187.
(10-352)**

Many patterns were so popular that they were
used in a variety of textile forms and worked in
different needlework techniques: contemporary
printed textiles, woven and quilted bedcovers, and
stenciled, painted, or embroidered bedcovers. A
quiltmaker might follow a popular pattern, but
render it using a different technique. Three bedcovers in Shelburne's collection feature the Oak
Leaf and Orange Slice pattern; two are worked in
appliqué with floral chintz fabric, while the third is
stenciled on white cloth.

**Appliquéd Quilt, Oak Leaf & Orange Slice
Pattern. 1840-1860. Made by Almira Letitia
Van Horn. Northeastern United States.
Cotton. 87" x 87". Gift of Mrs. Russell
Damon 1973-083. (10-555)**

This quilt was passed down through the female
descendants of Letitia van Horn to her great-
granddaughter, who presented it to the Museum.

**Appliquéd Quilt, Album Pattern. 1847-1850.
Maker unknown. Baltimore, Maryland.
Cotton. 94" x 110". Museum acquisition
1959. (10-330)**

The Ringgold quilt is an excellent example of the
elaborate sewing details, expensive fabrics, and
variety of patterns used in the Baltimore-style
album quilts. Major Ringgold was born in
Washington County, Maryland, in 1800, and graduated from West Point in 1818. He died in 1846
from a cannon ball wound he received at the bat-
tle of Palo Alto in the Mexican-American War. His
body was returned to Baltimore, where it was
buried with military honors.

Pieced and Appliquéd Quilt, Mariner's Compass Pattern. 1840-1860. Attributed to Emeline Barker (1820-1906). New York, New York. Cotton. 100" x 96". Museum acquisition 1952-545. (10-022)

The Compass pattern, distinguished by its circular pattern of radiating points, was used in American quiltmaking as early as 1834, and appears in an English patchwork quilt dated 1726. Variations of this popular quilt pattern appeared in the 1889 *Ladies' Art Catalog* and other late nineteenth- and early twentieth-century pattern books, under other names, including Sunburst and Sunflower.[4]

Florence Peto, who acquired this quilt and sold it to the Museum, described the border fabric as "blue Persian pear" in her book *American Quilts and Coverlets*.[5]

Pieced Quilt, Sawtooth Triangle Album Pattern. 1846. Made for Hannah Mather by members and friends of the Mitchell family of Attleboro, Pennsylvania and Ranacocus, New Jersey. Attleboro (now Langford), Pennsylvania. Cotton. 97" x 102". Museum acquisition. 1994-041. (10-753)

Hannah Mather married Joseph Paul Mitchell (b. 1820) in the 1840s. It is likely that friends and relatives made this quilt for the couple to celebrate that occasion, as the center block contains a pair of rings and a dove, a symbol of marriage. One of the blocks is inscribed: "To Hannah / Oh may thy future hours be given / to peace, to virtue, and to heaven / Thy hopes disdain a mortal birth / Thy joy ascend above the earth. / Eleanor Mather / Cheltenham / 1846." Other blocks contain detailed drawings of flowers, birds, landscape scenes, and such classical motifs as columns wrapped with vines and wreaths, and urns and baskets filled with flowers.

The Mitchells were Quakers, and this quilt relates in design to other quilts made in the Quaker community in eastern Pennsylvania and northern New Jersey. A descendant of Hannah Mitchell discovered this quilt in her grandmother's house.

Whole Cloth Quilt, White Floral Basket Pattern. 1852-1853. Made by Cornelia Thompson Noyes (1831-1862). Buffalo, New York. Cotton. 99" x 83". Museum acquisition 1958-212. (10-305)

Cornelia Thompson was born in 1831, the fourth child of Harry Thompson (1793-1873) and Catherine Curtiss Hull. In 1810 the Thompson family moved from Derby, Connecticut, to Black Rock, New York, now part of Buffalo. They built a house at 37 Ferry and Niagara Street. It is likely that Cornelia Noyes made this white-work quilt before or soon after her marriage in 1853 to Daniel Noyes, a lawyer from Laporte, Indiana.

The couple returned to Laporte to set up housekeeping and had one child in 1860, Richard Thompson Noyes, who died at birth. Two years later, Cornelia died suddenly at age thirty-one. She was buried near her parents' home in Buffalo.[6] Her husband returned her personal items to her family, including this white-work quilt. The quilt was passed down through the Thompson family, who presented it to the Museum.

Pieced Quilt, Double Sashed Diamond Pattern. 1855-1860. Made for Dorcas Eliza Meacham (b.1835). Galatia, New York. Cotton. 77" x 82". Gift of Agnes K. Lovell 1975-055. (10-573)

Dorcas Eliza Meacham was born in Galatia, New York in 1835, the daughter of Eleazer and Eliza Meacham. In 1850 she is listed in the New York census as living in Marathon with her parents, two brothers, and a hired hand on the family farm. By 1860 Dorcas is recorded as a member of R.M. Lovell's household, working as a housekeeper and caring for his two young children. She and Ransom Lovell (b.1823) married sometime in the 1850s and had six children. This quilt, signed by friends and Meacham family members, was probably made for Dorcas as a wedding present.

Pieced Quilt, Album Cross Pattern. 1851-1852. Made by Elizabeth Mary Powers Green (1822-1865). Keesville, New York. Silk. 88" x 87". Gift of Mr. & Mrs. Cecil Gilchrist 1975-012. (10-564)

Elizabeth Powers married Harry Green in 1845 in Keeseville, Clinton County, New York. She apparently asked her friends and relatives to sign small pieces of white silk, which she then pieced into this elegant quilt with scraps of dress goods. G.B. Cleaves wrote: "I send you this little block for you to look upon / That you may see my words when I am dead and gone." Frank of Wisconsin wrote: "When among the prairie flowers I tread, And seek a western home, My thoughts on you will often rest, And fondly whisper, come." Elizabeth signed one of the blocks herself and added this note: "Friends have combined to form / this beautiful spread / Of beauteous pattern and of / various shade / To join the whole my needle / has been true / In Eighteen Hundred Fifty / One and Two / Elizabeth M. Green / Christmas 1852."

Appliquéd and Embroidered Quilt, Tree of Life Medallion Pattern. 1850-1860. Made by Hannah Elizabeth Hamblin Delano. Ferrisburgh, Vermont. Cotton, cotton embroidery floss. 92" x 88". Museum acquisition 1994-16. (10-741)

This quilt is a unique combination of design motifs and quilt styles. The central medallion quilt pattern enjoyed a resurgence in popularity in the mid-nineteenth century. The Tree of Life pattern is very reminiscent of quilts and counterpanes made in the late eighteenth and early nineteenth centuries with large-scale flowering trees and bushes.

Hannah Elizabeth Hamblin was born in 1824 in Bridport, Vermont, the daughter of Alexander and Juliann Bishop Hamblin of Shoreham. In 1847 she married Nelson Delano, a farmer from Bridport, Vermont. This appliqué quilt, probably made by Hannah to set up housekeeping, was eventually given to their son, Noble G. Delano, a farmer in Shoreham, and his wife, Mary Sarah R. Durrin. Their child, Ida Mary Delano, who married Allen J. Larrow in 1908, inherited the Tree of Life quilt. Since the couple had no children, Ida gave the cherished quilt to her dear friend, Lydia Daniels.

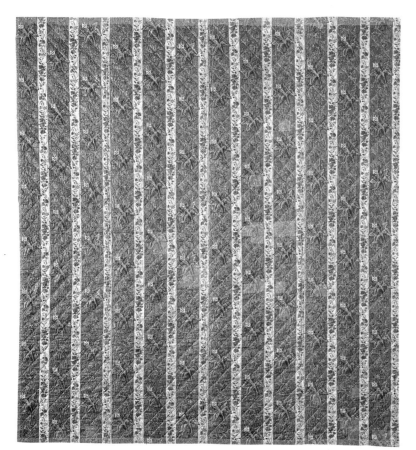

Whole Cloth Quilt, Chintz Stripes Pattern. 1830-1850. Made by Elizabeth East Root. Chester County, Pennsylvania. Cotton. 104" x 86". Gift of Elizabeth Parker 1993-032. (10-728)

This quilt, made with glazed floral chintz fabric, is an excellent example of the continued popularity of whole cloth quilts in the nineteenth century. The Museum was also given a Jacquard coverlet owned by Elizabeth Root.

Pieced and Appliquéd Quilt, Broken Star Pattern. 1860-1870. Made by Ellen Fullard Wright (1818-1889). Providence, Rhode Island. Cotton. 91" x 72". Museum acquisition 1991-029. (10-717)

Ellen Fullard was born in Bolton, Lancashire, England, and immigrated to America in 1842. She met and married James Hunter Wright (1813-1880), who was born in Dumfries, Scotland. By 1860 the Rhode Island census records the Wright household with James H. Wright, age 47, employed as an oyster fisherman; his wife Ellen, age 41; and their four children. By 1888 she was living with her daughter, Ellen Wright Fisher, in Stockport, New York. A letter from her son-in-law, George Fisher, mentions how Ellen F. Wright continued to sew in her declining years. He wrote, "Grandma is quite bright today, and has worked on her patchwork as though her life depended on it. She has not attempted to come down stairs today."[7]

Pieced Quilt, Log Cabin Barn Raising Pattern. 1870 -1874. Made by Bethia Willey Poor. Williamstown, Vermont. Cotton. 71" x 71". Gift of Mrs. J. S. Hockenberry 1970-125. (10-533)

Bethia Willey was born in 1820, the daughter of Benjamin and Clarissa Willey of Middlesex, Vermont. She married Gardner D. Poor, a farmer from Williamstown, Vermont (b.1813), on February 5, 1840. Their daughter Mary was born in 1843 and their son Edward J. in 1850. Bethia Poor died in 1894 at age seventy-four. It is likely this quilt was made as a wedding present for her son, who married in 1872, or her daughter, who married in 1875.

Pieced Quilt, Flying Geese Medallion. 1860-1880. Made by a member of the Brush family. Cambridge, Vermont. Cotton. 79" x 79". Museum acquisition 1991-56. (10-713)

This Flying Geese Medallion quilt and an older pieced wool quilt (10-714) were acquired by the Museum from the estate of a descendant of the Brush family of Cambridge. By the mid-1860s the number of Brush families had increased considerably from the original four families who settled there in the late 1700s. Of the fifteen women named Brush listed in the town, nine were old enough to be the maker of this quilt.

Appliquéd and Pieced Quilt, Centennial Album. 1876. Made by a member of the Burdick-Childs family. North Adams, Massachusetts. Cotton. 79 1/4" x 78 1/2". Museum acquisition 1987-040. (10-653)

The thirty-six blocks in this quilt illustrate scenes of family and home in North Adams and such biblical themes as Jonah and the whale. Two blocks were clearly inspired by the Centennial Exposition of 1876, which was widely published and illustrated in books and magazines. The appliquéd images of

Memorial Hall were familiar to most Americans of that day. Another exhibit building is framed with a banner that reads, "Declaration of Independence / Centennial Anniversary / 1776 / 1876."

It is believed that the quilt was made by a member of either the Childs or Burdick family. Preliminary research in Massachusetts identified a marriage between C. Edwin Childs and Alice Burdick in 1883 in North Adams, possibly the owners of this quilt.

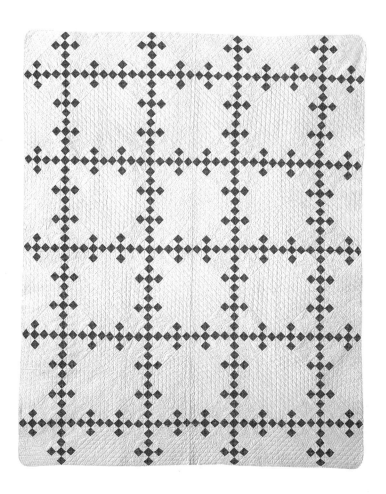

Pieced Quilt, Irish Chain Pattern. 1876. Made by Christina Bruns (b.1855). Huron, Ohio. Cotton. 82" x 67". Gift of Mrs. Robert H. Bruns 1970-013. (10-524)

Family information tells us that Mrs. Christina Bruns made this quilt when she was twenty-one years old to commemorate the 100th anniversary of the Signing of the Declaration of Independence. The Irish Chain pattern is one of the oldest patterns used in American quiltmaking.

Pieced and Appliquéd Quilt, Crazy Patchwork Pattern. 1870-1880. Made by Delphia Noice Haskins (1816-1892). Rochester, Vermont. Cotton. 82" x 69". Museum acquisition 1956-648. (10-215)

Delphia Ann Noice married Samuel Glover Haskins, a tailor from Dorchester, Massachusetts. In 1860 the couple was living in Rochester, Vermont, with their seven daughters, ages one to nineteen years old.

Delphia Haskins made two other appliquéd crazy quilts nearly identical to this quilt. One of them was probably made as a wedding present in 1877 for her daughter Ada.

When making her crazy quilt, Delphia Haskins chose to use plain and printed cotton fabrics for her quilt blocks, rather than the typical silks, satins, and velvets. She then decorated them with whimsical appliquéd images of deer, dogs, roosters, camels, and human figures.

Appliquéd Quilt, Rose & Bud Pattern. 1860-1870. Made by Elizabeth R. Colburn (b.1839). Pittsford, Vermont. Cotton. 91³/₄" x 89". Gift of Mr. & Mrs. Robert E. Degenhardt 1987-017. (10-652)

Elizabeth Ruth Colburn was born on February 19, 1839, the eldest daughter of Horace (b.1805) and Amaranth Smith (b.1811) of Pittsford, Vermont. The signature "E.R.Colburn" on the reverse of this quilt indicates that Elizabeth made this quilt before her first marriage in 1861 to a Mr. Aldrich. In 1873 she married William Eayres, a farmer. They lived with his parents, James and Anne Eayres, on the family farm in Pittsford.

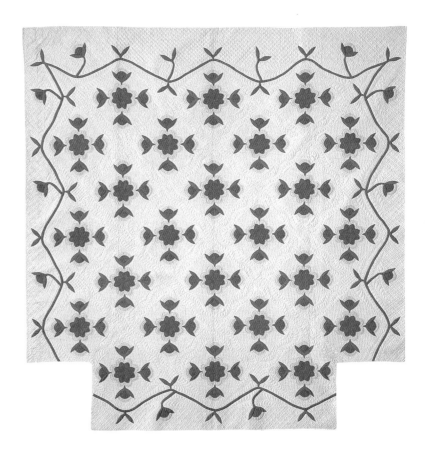

Eayres family, Pittsford, Vermont, c. 1877. Left to right: William Eayres, Elizabeth R. Colburn Eayres, James and Ann Eayres.

Pieced Quilt, Sunburst and Sawtooth Pattern. 1860-1870. Made by Eunice Hayes Baker Willard. Castleton, Vermont. Cotton. 89" x 81¹/₂". Museum acquisition 1954-454a. (10-166)

Eunice Hayes Baker Willard was born in Pawlet, Vermont, the daughter of Caroline Baker and Silas Willard (b.1780s). Willard, who served in the War of 1812, returned home in 1816 to marry Caroline Baker. They had five children, Cyrenius, Eunice, Emma A., Ella, and Catherine. Eunice later married a Mr. Euling. A note attached to the quilt described how her daughter, Mary Willard Euling Baldwin, presented the quilt to John and Mary (Miller) Baker. Later, it "...was drawn in lot by Fannie Baker—May 7, 1908."

Pieced Quilt, Random Star Pattern. 1870-1880. Maker unknown. Possibly from Vermont. Cotton; reverse: copperplate print *The Elopement*. 89" x 83½". Museum acquisition 1960-132. (10-379)

The abstract star pattern contains many fabrics printed in red-brown colorways popular in the 1870s. However, the copperplate print used as a backing fabric was made in the 1820s in England. The fabric had possibly served as bed hangings and when it was no longer needed, the fabric was reused by the quiltmaker to back this quilt. Electra H. Webb acquired this quilt for the copperplate toile on the reverse, not the abstract star quilt top.

Back of Random Star quilt above.

Pieced Quilt, Crossroads Pattern. 1880-1900. Made by Catherine Mary Severance Winchester. Middlebury, Vermont. Cotton. 92" x 92". Gift of John Winchester 1994-015. (10-734)

Catherine Severance learned to quilt from her mother. When Catherine died at age ninety-three, she left a legacy of a trunk filled with quilts. Just before her ninetieth birthday, She wrote an auto-biography entitled *Recollections of a Long Life*, which included many stories of her mother's quiltmaking activity.

Pieced and Painted Quilt, Crazy Patchwork Pattern. 1870-1880. Made by Catherine Mary Severance Winchester (1821-1915). Middlebury, Vermont. Silk, velvet, and satin. 71 1/2" x 72". Gift of Alice Winchester 1992-36. (10-719)

Catherine Severance was born in 1821 to Ebenezer (1791-1880) and Corcina Jones Severance, farmers in Middlebury, Vermont. In 1848 Catherine married Reverend Warren Winchester (1823-1889), who served as pastor of several churches in New Hampshire and Massachusetts. The couple had eleven children, but only the youngest, Benjamin, grew to be an adult. After her husband died, Catherine Winchester went to live with her son Benjamin and traveled with him to Alaska, Washington, and then Germany, where he too studied for the ministry.

Catherine Winchester was an accomplished artist and enjoyed painting landscape scenes and still-life compositions. She also loved to quilt, and combined her two interests in this exceptional quilt.

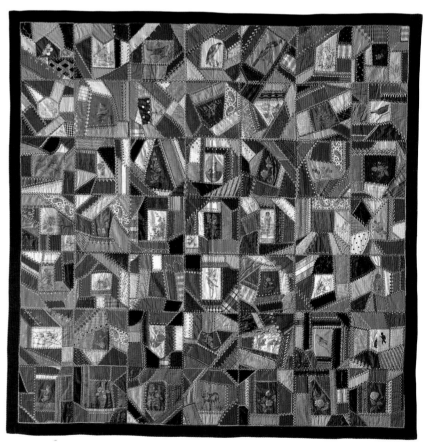

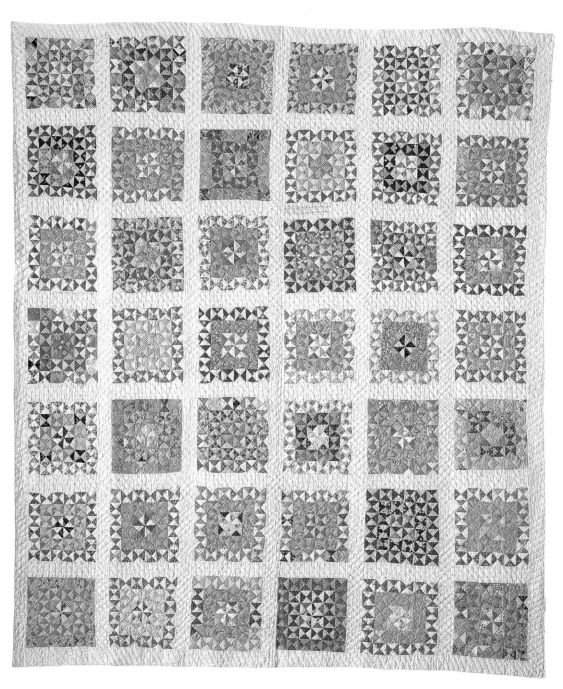

**Pieced Quilt, Windmill Blades Pattern.
1885-1890. Made by Clarissa White Alford
(1806-1890). Vermont. Cotton. 87" x 75".
Gift of Miss Delia B. Alford 1961-083. (10-399)**

Clarissa White, born in 1806 in Cavendish, Vermont,
married Ami Alford in 1832. Clarissa raised seven
sons and two daughters, plus the six children from
her husband's first marriage. The 1860 national
census records the Alford family living in Waterville,
Vermont. Sometime after that Clarissa moved to
Quebec to live with one of her daughters. This
quilt, made in the last years of Clarissa Alford's life,

was given her to younger son, A.G. Alford, who
passed it on to his daughter, Delia B. Alford.

The white and black floral print cloth used for
the sashing and border is print #2746 manufactured by the Cocheco Print Works on July 6, 1876.
Another print, brown acorns on a white ground, is
identified as print #522, also by Cocheco and
printed February 13, 1884. The quilt is made of 42
squares, each made of 144 triangles, for a total of
6,048 pieces.

Right: Clarissa White Alford

Pieced Quilt, Log Cabin Windmill Pattern. 1880-1900. Made by Josephine Mary Cushman Carpenter (1851-1912). East Charlotte, Vermont. Cotton with red wool central squares. 83" x 68". Museum acquisition 1954-421. (10-133)

Josephine Mary Cushman was born in Middlebury, Vermont, the daughter of Angelica Cushman. Josephine married Joseph Carpenter (b.1845), a laborer from Vergennes, Vermont, in 1867. Joseph took up farming in East Charlotte, Vermont, and the couple had four children.

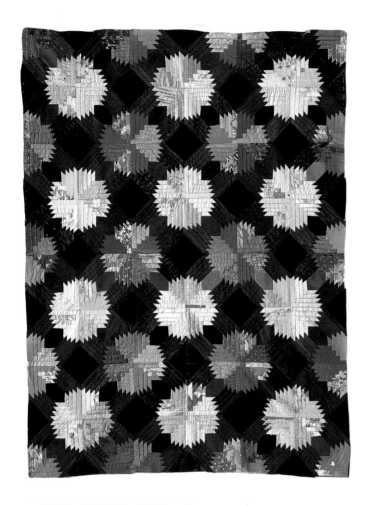

Pieced Quilt Top, Log Cabin Sunburst Pattern. 1880-1900. Made by Ella Holcombe (1872-1957). Bridport, Vermont. Silk, satin. 54³/₄" x 41". Gift of Barbara Smith 1990-022. (10-702)

Ella Holcombe was born in 1872, the daughter of Wilbur (1810-1916) and Mary Livermore Holcombe (1845-1936), who operated a farm in West Addison, Vermont. Ella was educated in Middlebury, and taught school in Bridport. She later devoted herself to historical and genealogical research. She joined the New England Historic Genealogical Society in 1945, and compiled extensive information about the Holcombe family. Ella Holcombe died in 1957, and is buried in the Bridport cemetery.

Ella Holcombe with her students

Pieced Quilt, Tumbler Pattern. 1880-1930. Made by a member of the Almy family. Fall River, Massachusetts. Cotton. 66" x 60". Gift of Linda and Stafford Almy 1987-49.1. (10-654).

In the late 1880s several cotton print manufacturers featured cotton furnishing prints with scenes of country life—floral landscapes with children at play, hunting scenes with men and hounds, couples playing tennis, and bucolic scenes which presented an idealized view of life before railroads, steam power, and modern urban life. The scale of these furnishing prints was often too large to be used for piecework quilts. However, the maker of this tumbler quilt carefully cut out smaller motifs from printed cotton to feature in her quilt: prancing horses, dogs, a cat in a basket, and circus performers. The fabrics for this quilt might have been produced by American Print Works or Bay State Print Works, two of the many textile mills operating in Fall River in the late nineteenth century.[8]

**Pieced and Embroidered Quilt, Crazy
Patchwork Pattern. 1894. Made by Jeanette
Brooks Spaulding Wright (b.1834).
Indianapolis, Indiana. Silk satin, velvet, taffeta,
and jacquard-woven. 74" x 55". Gift of Mrs.
Jeanette Sharp Andrus 1984-54. (10-618)**

Jeanette Brooks Spaulding, born in Claremont,
New Hampshire, married Sheffield Hayward
Wright of St. Johnsbury, Vermont. They lived much
of their lives in Indianapolis. Mrs. Wright and her
friends made this quilt as a wedding present for
her daughter, Nettie H. Wright. Nettie later gave

the quilt to her daughter, Jeanette Sharp Andrus,
who in turn presented it to the Museum.

This quilt illustrates the elaborate handwork
often used to decorate patchwork crazy quilts.
Each of the twelve pattern blocks was pieced,
embroidered, and/or painted before the quilt was
assembled. Other designs on the quilt include children at play, a spider web, and Little Bo Peep.
Needlework techniques include ribbon and bead-
work, appliqué, outline and chenille embroidery, as
well as herringbone and feather stitching along the
seams.

Pieced Quilt, Red Pinwheel Pattern. 1880-1900. Made by Margaret H. Cunningham (b. 1840s). Cabot, Vermont. Cotton. 76 1/2" x 74". Gift of Marion Urie 1995. (10-748)

The Cunningham sisters, Margaret and Jenette, never married and lived with their brother, David, on the family farm. Their ancestors were trained weavers from Paisley, Scotland, who immigrated to Massachusetts in the early 1800s to work in the textile industry. The family later moved to Vermont to farm. Both of these quilts and a pair of paisley shawls were inherited by their nephew, Corey W. Urie, and then by his daughter, Marion V. Urie.

Pieced Quilt, Yellow Pinwheel Pattern. 1880-1900. Made by Jenette Cunningham (b. 1840s). Cabot, Vermont. Cotton. 76 1/2" x 74". Gift of Marion Urie 1995-19. (10-749)

Pieced Quilt, Figural Mosaic Pattern. 1880-1920. Maker unknown. Ballston Spa, New York. Cotton. 89" x 87". Museum acquisition 1996-14. (10-754)

This quilt was found in a trunk that belonged to the Palmer family, who had lived in the Ballston Spa area since the late 1880s. The presence of African-American figures in the quilt is unusual and might indicate that the bedcover was made by a member of an African-American community. Research has identified the existence of an African-American Odd Fellows Lodge in the Ballston Spa area.

Appliquéd and Embroidered Counterpane, Whirling Peacock Medallion. 1880-1910. Maker unknown. Possibly from Pennsylvania. Cotton prints appliquéd on a linen ground. 104 1/2" x 100". Gift of Electra H. Webb 1952. (10-090)

The bird motifs appliquéd on this quilt resemble the designs used in Pennsylvania German woodcarvings and fractur paintings.

1 9 2 0 - 1 9 5 0

Appliquéd Quilt, Wind-Blown Tulips. 1930-1940. Made by Olga Six Baker. Detroit, Michigan. Cotton. 88" x 87". Gift of Olga Six Baker 1991-39. (10-711)

Olga Six was born in Alorton, Illinois, attended Northwestern University and studied abroad. She was teaching school in Detroit when she made this quilt in the 1930s and won many prizes at local needlecraft fairs for her workmanship. After her marriage to Earl B. Baker, she moved to Baxter, Georgia in 1935 where she and her husband operated Bay Creek Farm and Pine Lodge Court. She was very involved in her community: a charter member of the Business and Professional

Women's Club and President of the Women's Club, the Pilot Club, and the local chapter of the Eastern Star.

Olga Six Baker

Appliquéd Quilt, Currants and Coxcomb Pattern. 1930-1940. Made by Vera Bryant Woodward (d.1960s). Dayton, Ohio, or Lowell, Massachusetts. Cotton. 84" x 84". Gift of Franklin B. Smith 1986-053. (10-644)
Vera Bryant was born in Dayton, Ohio, her family being among the founders of that city. Her husband, Luther Woodward, was a professor in Lowell, Massachusetts. The couple lived in New England for many years and retired to St. Petersburg, Florida. The donor, Franklin B. Smith, inherited the collection of six quilts after his great-aunt's death.

WILD GOOSE CHASE VARIATION

This stunning quilt was pieced entirely from silk and satin fabrics. The deep saturated color in the outer blocks surrounds the royal blues located in the center rows. To add even more contrast to the quilt, the creator pieced the background triangles in black. Although most of the three-geese blocks are made from the same fabrics, many have multiple fabrics within the block. This quilt is comprised of about three hundred different fabrics.

A variation on the Wild Goose Chase block, this quilt is made of 168 Flying Geese blocks. Each block consists of three "geese" for a grand total of 504 flying geese, 1008 background triangles, and 336 sashing strips. The entire quilt top measures 64 1/2" x 54".

The Flying Geese units are turned vertically and horizontally to create an appealing pattern of color and symmetry. The "geese" units are separated by a wonderful assortment of sashings in woven, striped, and solid fabrics characteristic of that time.

The back of this quilt is a seamless maroon cotton sateen. The front and back of the quilt have been turned into each other and machine stitched, with the row of stitching showing on the quilt front. The filling is a thin cotton batt. The ties of heavy black waxed cotton thread were knotted on the back of the quilt.

The following instructions are a close rendering of the original quilt, using our modern day quick-piecing techniques. Directions will be given for rotary cutting and machine piecing. Templates for hand piecing are also included.

SUPPLIES

Use a variety of silk necktie fabrics for the flying geese blocks. Add bright colored silks for sparkle and contrast. The fabric requirements below give the total yardage needed.

> 3 1/2 yards background fabric
> 2 1/2 yards geese fabric
> 1 3/4 yards sashing fabric
> 3 1/2 yards backing fabric
> 1 spool black perle cotton *or*
>   3 skeins embroidery floss
> 3/4 yard for the binding
> thin cotton batting

Preparing Recycled Ties for the Quilt

1. Carefully take apart the ties.
2. Remove the lining and interfacing.
3. Wash ties in a mild detergent by hand. If a silk tie continues to bleed, eliminate it.
4. Line dry and press on silk setting.
5. Check for spots or worn places that are not usable.
6. Check the backs, which may be more interesting than the fronts.
7. If the silk is unstable, you can interface it for ease in handling.

FLYING GEESE BLOCKS

CUTTING

This method for making Flying Geese was developed by Laura Nownes, who with Diana McClun wrote *Quilts Quilts, and More Quilts*. Cut all the fabrics from the straight of grain.

- Cut forty-eight 2"-wide strips from the background fabric. Cut every 2" to make 1008 2" squares. Set aside.
- Cut 2"-wide strips from the assorted "geese" fabrics. Cut these strips into 3 1/2"-long segments. You will need 504 units. One segment yields one unit; three units comprise a block.
- Cut 336 1 1/4" x 5" strips from the sashing fabrics.

**Pieced and Hand Tied Quilt, Wild Goose
Chase Variation, 1875-1890. Maker unknown.
Attributed to Vermont. Silk brocades,
jacquard patterns. 64 $\frac{1}{2}$" x 54". Gift of Mrs.
Wescott 1959. (10-354)**

Detail of *Wild Goose Chase Variation*

CONSTRUCTION

PIECING THE BLOCKS

1. With right sides together, place a 2" square on a 2" x 3½" rectangle with the corners matching. If you are concerned about sewing a straight line, mark a diagonal line from corner to corner on the wrong side of the 2" squares.
2. If the silk fabric is slippery, pin.
3. Sew from corner to corner.

4. Fold back the square to check for accuracy.
5. Cutting through both layers, trim the excess. Press.

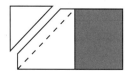

6. Repeat for the other side.

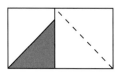

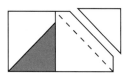

7. Press in the direction of the arrows.

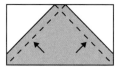

This completes one unit.

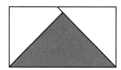

8. Complete three "geese" units.

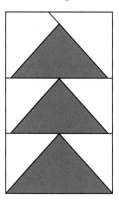

9. Select two 1¼" x 5" strips from the sashing fabrics.
10. Piece a sashing strip to each side of the geese units to complete a block.

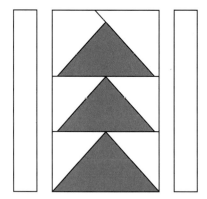

There are 168 Flying Geese blocks in the quilt.

PIECING THE ROWS

The Flying Geese "fly" right in all except rows 4 and 5.

1. Arrange the blocks as shown in the following diagram.
2. Using a ¼" seam allowance, piece twelve blocks together to make row 1.
3. Alternating the direction of the beginning block, piece row 2.

You will piece seven of row 1 and seven of row 2, for a total of fourteen rows.

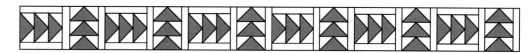

4. Pin at intersections.

5. Using a $1/4$" seam allowance, piece the rows together.

PIECING THE QUILT BACKING

Unless you are using a very wide sateen or lightweight upholstery fabric to closely replicate the original, you will need to piece the back.

1. Cut the $3 1/2$-yard backing fabric in half.

2. Trim the selvages from the edges.

3. Sew together on the longer edge with a $1/4$" seam allowance.

4. Press the seam to one side.

TIEING OR QUILTING

1. Turn the quilt top over and gently press.

2. Layer the quilt top, batting, and backing fabric. Baste.

3. Using perle cotton or embroidery floss, tie the quilt at the intersection of the sashings. The original quilt is tied on the back. Refer to a basic quiltmaking book for this procedure, if needed.

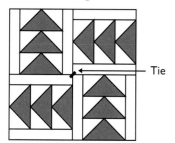

Tie

4. If you prefer a quilted top, hand or machine quilt.

BINDING

Yardage for a $1/4$"-wide finished, straight-grain, double-fold binding is included in the fabric requirements. This type of binding will wear better than turning the quilt top and backing fabric into each other as was done on the original quilt.

1. Cut six 2"-wide strips across the width of the fabric for the binding. Sew the strips together end to end using a diagonal seam. Trim seam allowance to a $1/4$".

2. Fold and press the strip in half lengthwise. Align the raw edges of the folded strip with the edge of the quilt. Using a $1/4$" seam allowance, sew the binding strip to the top of the quilt. Bring the folded edge of the binding strip to the back of the quilt and stitch it down.

3. Add a label with your name, address, name of the quilt, year the quilt was completed, and any other important information.

TEMPLATES

Templates do not include seam allowances.

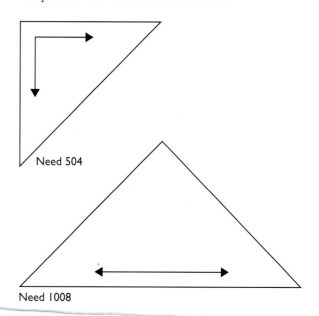

Need 504

Need 1008

Need 336

THE SUNFLOWER QUILT

*T*his *Sunflower* quilt is a striking example of the perennial sunflower motif. This interpretation of the sunflower was created by Carrie M. Carpenter, whose inscription appears on the back.

The *Sunflower* quilt measures approximately 78" x 84", including a 14" drop. Three stuffed stalks of sunflowers are hand appliquéd to twenty-eight panels of white cotton background. Thirty-two bright yellow-orange sunflowers with reverse appliquéd brown centers and sixty-two green leaves and their adjoining stems cover the top.

The background is hand quilted in a chevron pattern. Small quilted flower motifs are nestled in the V created by the stems. The veins of the leaves are quilted with green thread and the flower centers are quilted with brown thread.

The following instructions are a close rendering of the original quilt. Instructions are also given for a 78" x 84" quilt without the drop cut-outs. (Instructions for making the quilt without cut-outs are given in parentheses.)

Caroline Carpenter was born in 1835, the daughter of Roswell, Jr. and Philura Kinsman Carpenter, of Northfield, Vermont. They lived on the farm her grandfather, Roswell Carpenter had established in 1787, when he moved to Vermont from Charleston, New Hampshire.

Carrie, as she was known by her family, married William L. Smith in 1861. They had a daughter, Gertie C. Williams in 1867. One year later William Smith died in an accident. In 1877 Carrie remarried Amasa Persons, a farmer from Northfield.

Many women were involved in the temperance movement at that time. In 1878 Carrie was appointed Superintendent of the Northfield Juvenile Temple, an organization dedicated to providing a temperance education for children. The meeting notes recorded that the Temple boasted 150 members, all "working zealously for Temperance."[1]

SUPPLIES

5 1/2 yards for background fabric and binding
4 yards for stalks, stems, and leaves
1 1/2 yards for sunflowers
1/2 yard for sunflower centers
4 1/2 yards for quilt backing
thin cotton batting

SUNFLOWER QUILT TOP

CUTTING

Cutting instructions are given for the quilt with and without cut-outs. Follow the cutting instructions in parentheses if you are making the quilt without cut-outs.

- **Panels:** Cut 22 (24) 14 1/2" square panels of background fabric for the panels. Cut 6 (6) 14 1/2" x 22" panels of background fabric for the panels.
- **Stalks:** Cut 3 strips at least 76" x 3 1/2" from the length of the fabric on the straight of grain for the stalks.
- **Leaves:** Trace 62 (66) leaves using Template A. Add a 3/16" seam allowance when cutting for appliquéing.

- **Stems:** Use the remaining fabric for 3/8" finished bias strips. You will need approximately 936" or 26 yards of bias. Two methods to consider are the continuous bias strip method, or bias bars. The width you cut your strips depends on which method you choose. The continuous bias method allows you to machine stitch one side and hand or machine appliqué the opposite side. Refer to Harriet Hargrave's *Heirloom Machine Quilting* for more information on the continuous bias method. The bias bar method works well for hand appliqué. Refer to a basic quiltmaking book for further instructions on the bias bar method.
- **Sunflowers:** Trace 32 (34) sunflowers using Template B. Add a 3/16" seam allowance when cutting for appliquéing. (The center and cutting line for reverse appliqué need to be marked on the template.)
- **Sunflower centers:** Cut 32 (34) 4" squares for the sunflower centers. The center of the sunflower is reverse appliquéd.

Appliquéd Quilt, Sunflower Pattern. 1870-1890. Made by Caroline (Carrie) Carpenter. Northfield, Vermont. Cotton. 78" x 84". Gift of Ethel Washburne 1987-019. (10-651)

Need 11 (12)   Need 11 (12)   Need 2 (3)   Need 3 (3)   Need 1 (0)

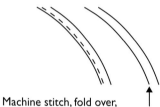

Machine stitch, fold over, and appliqué.

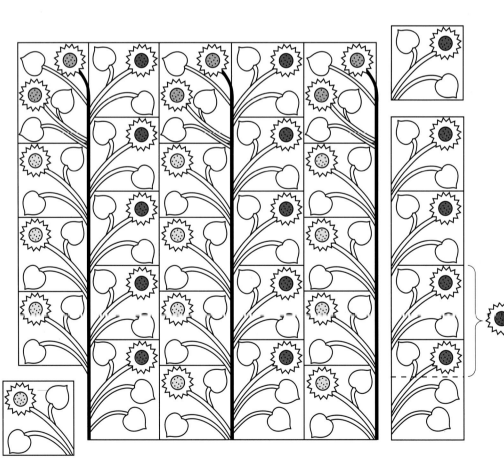

There are five different layouts for the appliqué designs. Refer to the following diagram for the placement of appliqué shapes on the panels.

APPLIQUÉING THE PANELS

1. Appliqué the bias stems onto the panels using the diagram for placement. Start with the shortest stem. The stem of the leaf at the bottom of each panel crosses the seam allowance when the panels are pieced (see page 85). You can leave the end free and appliqué after piecing the rows. Notice the ends of the stems will be covered by the stalk. Stop appliquéing 1/2" from the edge of the

panel; this keeps the stems out of your seam allowance. These raw edges will be covered by the stalks.

2. Appliqué the leaves. Keep the leaf shape inside the seam allowance.

3. Cut out the center of the sunflower following the cutting line on Template B. Place the brown center fabric behind the hole you have created. Reverse appliqué the sunflower to the underlying brown center. Turn the sunflower over and trim the excess.

4. Position the sunflowers as shown in the diagrams. Appliqué them to the panels using a 3/16" seam allowance. The three sunflowers at the top of the stalks will be added after the stalks are appliquéd.

ASSEMBLING THE QUILT

1. Arrange the panels using the following diagram.

2. Using a 1/4" seam allowance, piece the panels into vertical rows. Press.

3. Piece row 1 to row 2, row 3 to row 4, and row 5 to row 6. Press.

4. Appliqué the stem of the leaf at the bottom of each panel over the seamline.

5. Add three 1 1/2" wide finished stalks to the quilt top. Press the stalk fabric in half lengthwise. Starting at the bottom, place the raw edges of the stalk fabric 1/2" from the seam.

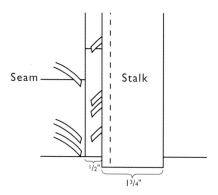

Seam ─── Stalk

1/2"

1 3/4"

6. Place a mark on your panel where the stalk curves to make the stalk for the sunflower.

7. Sew a 1/4" seam to the mark. Repeat for rows 3 and 4, and rows 5 and 6.

8. The stalks on the original sunflower quilt are stuffed. As you appliqué down the open side, lightly stuff with cotton or polyester batting.

9. Curve, stuff, and appliqué the stalk toward the sunflower.

10. Appliqué the three remaining sunflowers.

11. Assemble the rows to complete the quilt top.

Detail of *Sunflower* quilt

QUILTING

The background quilting in the *Sunflower* quilt is done in a chevron pattern. In contrast to the background quilting are a vast array of little free-form flowers quilted in the V created by the stems. The beautiful quilting averages eleven stitches to the inch. The sunflower leaves have a maple leaf shape quilted in the center of them. The sunflower is quilted around the outside of the center circle with a half-egg-shaped design. The center of the sunflower is a 1/2" grid.

1. Turn the quilt over and press.

2. Mark the quilt top as shown in the diagrams below.

3. Layer the quilt top, batting, and backing. Baste.

4. Quilt the three layers together.

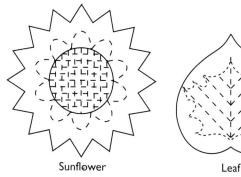

Sunflower   Leaf

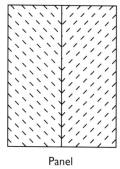

Panel

BINDING

Yardage for a 1/4"-wide finished, straight-grain, double-fold binding is included in the fabric requirements. This type of binding will wear better than turning the back to the front as was done on the original quilt.

1. Cut eight 2"-wide strips across the width of the fabric for the binding. Sew the strips together end to end using a diagonal seam. Trim seam allowance to 1/4".

2. Fold and press the strip in half lengthwise. Align the raw edges of the folded strip with the edge of the quilt. Using a 1/4" seam allowance, sew the binding strip to the top of the quilt. Bring the folded edge of the binding strip to the back of the quilt and stitch it down.

3. Add a label with your name, address, name of the quilt, year the quilt was completed, and any other important information.

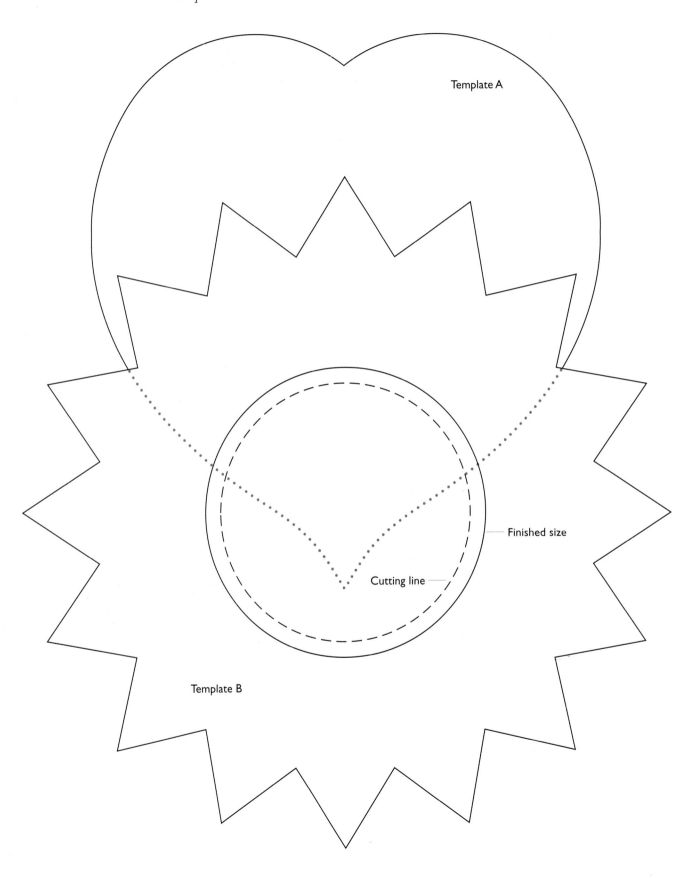

Template A

Finished size

Cutting line

Template B

**Pieced and Appliquéd Quilt, Calico Garden.
1952. Made by Florence Peto (1881-1970).
Tenafly, New Jersey. Nineteenth- and twentieth-century cottons. 49" x 39". Museum
acquisition 1952-548. (10-025)**

CALICO GARDEN

This charming crib-size quilt was made in 1952 from a variety of eighteenth- and nineteenth-century fabrics, hand-blocked and copperplate prints, chintzes, and other English and French calicoes. The original quilt measures 49" x 39".

The center section is comprised of forty-eight Nine Patch blocks set on point with alternating appliqué blocks. The center section is appliquéd to border strips and mitered at the corners. The four corner blocks are appliquéd onto the background fabric over the mitered seam. Cut-out appliqué and one-inch squares on point are appliquéd onto the border.

The following instructions are a close rendering of the original quilt.

Well-known as an author, scholar, and historian, Florence Peto was also an accomplished quiltmaker. *Calico Garden* is one of the many quilts for which she won prizes at state competitions. She described the quilt in a letter to the Museum in 1951: "It has always been my desire to preserve fascinating old fabrics. One time I bought up whole cartons of scraps —none of [which] were over two inches square! But they were charming, . . . obviously handsome examples of early hand-blocking and early copperplates as well as English and French calicoes. *Calico Garden* was [made] to use up the tiny pieces. ([A]ll the little designs are original with me.) I made the little quilt first and later, from the rest of the fabrics, a large quilt. . . . I called it a 'Mother and Daughter set' . . . All the materials are old except the white broadcloth background and the small flowered yellow backing."[2]

Florence Peto

SUPPLIES

Use a variety of fabrics for the Nine Patch blocks and appliqué designs. Choose some fabrics with flowers and leaves for the cut-out appliqué technique. The fabric requirements below give the total yardage needed.

3 yards background fabric for the alternate appliqué blocks and borders
2 yards assorted fabrics for Nine Patch blocks and appliqué designs
1 ½ yards backing fabric
½ yard binding fabric
thin cotton batting

NINE PATCH BLOCKS

This sparkling little quilt contains an inordinate number of fabrics. With some exceptions, a combination of three fabrics were used in each block. If you are using a wide variety of fabrics, you need to cut individual squares. The placement of light, medium, and dark fabrics creates interest and contrast. Mrs. Peto used the center of the Nine Patch to show interesting details in the fabrics.

CUTTING

Cut all the fabrics from the straight of grain.

- Cut 544 1 ½" squares from an assortment of light, medium, and dark fabrics. (This includes 112 squares for the appliqué border.)

PIECING THE BLOCKS

1. Refer to the quilt for placement of light, medium, and dark fabrics.
2. Follow the piecing sequence below for one Nine Patch block. The arrows indicate which direction to press. You will need forty-eight Nine Patch blocks in all.

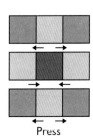 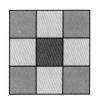

Press

APPLIQUE BLOCKS

There are thirty-nine template patterns for the appliqué blocks (thirty-five blocks for the center section and four "optional" blocks for the corner blocks in the border). Line drawings for each appliqué block are given at 1 ½". Enlarge the patterns 200% on a copy machine for the 3" finished block.

CUTTING

- Cut thirty-nine 4" squares from the background fabric. You will size them down to 3 ½" after you finish appliquéing the block.

- Make templates and cut the individual shapes adding a $3/16$" seam allowance from selected fabrics for each of the thirty-nine blocks.

APPLIQUÉING THE DESIGNS

1. Determine which shapes will overlap other shapes, and place them onto the background fabric.

2. Appliqué the shapes onto the 4" blocks.

3. When you have appliquéd all thirty-nine blocks, cut the blocks down to $3 1/2$".

Detail of *Calico Garden*

ASSEMBLING THE ROWS

1. Arrange the blocks as shown in the following diagram. Note they are set on point.

2. Piece the Nine Patch blocks and alternating appliqué blocks into rows using a $1/4$" seam allowance.

3. Press the seams in the same direction within each row, pressing every alternating row so the seam allowances lay the opposite direction. This will make it easier for seams to nest together and eliminate bulk. Pin at intersections if needed.

4. Using a $1/4$" seam allowance, join the rows as shown in the diagram, aligning seams. Start and stop $1/4$" from the edge to allow for the seam allowance needed when appliquéing the entire center

section to the borders. Piece the two halves and then sew the halves together.

5. Press the entire center section.

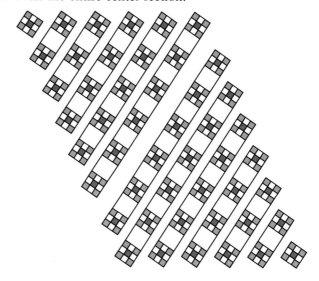

The border on the *Calico Garden* features cut-out appliqué swags, four appliquéd corner blocks, and one inch squares on point appliquéd to the background fabric.

CUTTING

In the original quilt the center section was appliquéd to four border strips. Following are instructions for that method. (You may choose to hand or machine appliqué the center section to a $1 1/2$-yard piece of background fabric and size to 49" x 39".)

- Cut two 10" x 73" strips of the background fabric for the side borders.

- Cut two 11" x 65" strips of the background fabric for the top and bottom borders.

- Cut floral motifs from printed fabrics for the broderie perse appliqué swags in the border.

ADDING THE BORDER

1. Find and match the centers of each border to the center units.

2. Appliqué the center unit to the top, bottom, and side borders, stopping short at the corners to allow for mitering.

3. Fold the borders right sides together, mark the 45° angle, and sew the seam to create a mitered corner. Trim to $1/4$" and press.

APPLIQUÉING THE BORDER

Cut-out appliqué is a simple technique of cutting a flower, leaf, fruit, or other printed motif from the fabric and appliquéing its shape to create a new design. The borders in the *Calico Garden* use cut-out appliqué to create swags. The corner blocks are also appliquéd to the borders. You may wish to appliqué the designs directly onto the background fabric.

1. Mark reference points on the borders to indicate the finished size. (You will size the borders down after you have appliquéd the shapes onto the fabric.)

2. Refer to the following diagram for placement of the cut-out appliqué swags, corner blocks, and squares on point.

3. Arrange the cut-out appliqué motifs on the top, bottom, sides, and corners of the border fabric. Appliqué them using your preferred method.

4. Appliqué the corner squares onto the background fabric. (Or appliqué the shapes directly to the border.)

5. Appliqué the 1 1/2" squares on point, twenty-four across the top and bottom borders and thirty-one along the side borders, leaving 1/4" on the outer edge to add the binding. NOTE: You will turn under 1/4" for a 1" finished square.

6. Size quilt to 49" high x 39" wide.

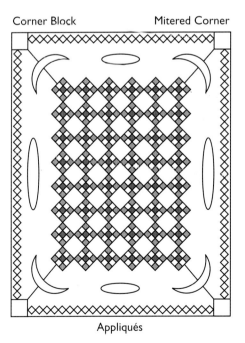

Corner Block   Mitered Corner

Appliqués

QUILTING

The quilting design for the *Calico Garden* is a cross-hatch pattern with outline quilting around the appliqué designs.

1. Mark the top for quilting as shown in the diagram below.

2. Layer top, batting, and back. Baste.

3. Quilt the three layers together.

Quilting design for border. Lines are 1/2" apart.

Quilting design for Nine Patch blocks.

BINDING

Yardage for a 1/4"-wide finished, straight-grain, double-fold binding is included in the fabric requirements. This type of binding will wear better than turning the back to the front as was done on the original quilt.

1. Cut five 2"-wide strips across the width of the fabric for the binding. Sew the strips together end to end using a diagonal seam. Trim seam allowance to a 1/4".

2. Fold and press the strip in half lengthwise. Align the raw edges of the folded strip with the edge of the quilt. Using a 1/4" seam allowance, sew the binding strip to the top of the quilt. Bring the folded edge of the binding strip to the back of the quilt and stitch it down.

3. Add a label with your name, address, name of the quilt, year the quilt was completed, and any other important information.

*Templates do not include seam allowances.
See photocopy permission on page 2.*

Enlarge 200% on a
copy machine for a
3" finished block.

Enlarge 200% on a
copy machine for a
3" finished block.

Enlarge 200% on a
copy machine for a
3" finished block.

Corner block

Corner block

Corner block

Corner block

THE SARAH JOHNSON QUILT

Sarah Johnson was born in 1812 to John and Hannah Johnson of Cochranville, Pennsylvania. In 1845 she married John Holcombe of Bucks County, and they took up farming in Lancaster County. Sarah, who had no children, enjoyed playing accordion and making quilts. Upon her death, she bequeathed nine of her quilts to relatives and the remainder to her husband.

Quilts made in the Lancaster area often contain German folk designs. One of the oldest designs is the *fylfot*, or pinwheel motif, which is thought to represent good and evil. The prominent inclusion of the *fylfot* in the center medallion of this quilt illustrates the assimilation of German folk designs in the non-German community.[3]

This intricate scrap quilt is full of wonderful details. The focus of the quilt is a center medallion and the blocks radiating from it. The center medallion consists of four Variable Star blocks and five alternate blocks with charming appliqué designs. It is surrounded by several borders. The remaining 4" Variable Stars are set in straight rows with alternate blocks around the center medallion. Six block variations radiate from the corners of the center medallion, creating an interesting secondary pattern. A Flying Geese border flies around three sides, and a striped fabric finishes the quilt. The finished dimensions are 92" x 89".

The following instructions are a close rendering of the original quilt. Any block size variance in the original version has been standardized.

SUPPLIES

4 1/2 yards background fabric
4 1/2 yards assorted fabrics for the stars, appliqués, pieced medallion borders, and Flying Geese border
1/4 yard floral fabric
1 1/2 yards for the outside border (or 3 yards if you do not want to piece the outside border). The original quilt has a striped border.
8 yards backing fabric
1/2 yard fabric binding
thin cotton batting

APPLIQUÉ BLOCKS

There are thirteen appliqué blocks in the Sarah Johnson quilt; five are in the center medallion and eight are in the body of the quilt. There are also appliquéd circles scattered across the quilt. If you want to include these circles, refer to the picture for placement. They appear to be part of the fabric, but are actually appliquéd to the quilt.

CUTTING

- Cut thirteen 5" squares from the background fabric. (After you complete the appliqué, size the block to 4 1/2".)
- Trace the appliqué shapes using Templates A–H. Add a 3/16" seam allowance when cutting for appliquéing.

APPLIQUÉING THE BLOCKS

1. Appliqué using the following diagrams for placement.

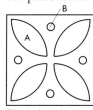

Block 1, Make 1

Block 2, Make 1

Block 3, Make 1

Block 4, Make 1

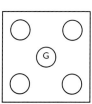

Block 5, Make 6

Block 6, Make 2

VARIABLE STARS

There are 172 4" Variable Stars in the quilt. Four of the stars are in the center medallion. The two stars are in the Flying Geese border are 3 1/2" Variable Stars. Templates S, T, U, and V are given for the 3 1/2" Variable Stars. The center of the star is almost

**Pieced Quilt, Stars and Pinwheel Medallion.
1826. Made by Sarah Johnson (1812-1876),
marked "No.4, 1826." Southern Lancaster
County, Pennsylvania. Cotton. 92" x 89".
Museum acquisition 1958-82.10. (10-283)**

always the background fabric. The star points are a dark fabric and the rest of the star block is a medium-value fabric. The stars can be quick-pieced.

CUTTING

- Cut one $2\frac{1}{2}$" square from the background fabric for the star center.
- Cut four $1\frac{1}{2}$" squares from a medium value fabric for the corners.
- Cut four $1\frac{1}{2}$" x $2\frac{1}{2}$" rectangles from the same medium value fabric, and eight $1\frac{1}{2}$" squares from a dark fabric for the star points.

PIECING THE STARS

1. With right sides together, place a $1\frac{1}{2}$" square on a $1\frac{1}{2}$" x $2\frac{1}{2}$" rectangle, with corners matching.

2. Sew from corner to corner.

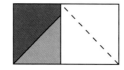

3. Fold back the square to check for accuracy.

4. Cutting through both layers, trim the excess. Press. Repeat for the other side. This is the star point. Piece four for one star.

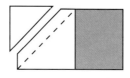

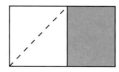

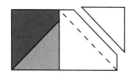

5. Add a $1\frac{1}{2}$" square to each end of one star point. Repeat.

6. Piece a star point to the center $2\frac{1}{2}$" square. Repeat on the other side. Add the star points and corner squares to complete one star.

7. Using different fabrics, make 172 stars.

8. Using the templates, construct two $3\frac{1}{2}$" Variable Stars for the bottom border.

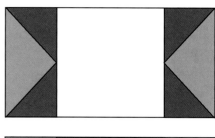

ALTERNATE BLOCKS

CUTTING

There are 160 $4\frac{1}{2}$" background squares in the quilt. The original quilt has four background squares cut from a floral fabric.

- Cut 156 $4\frac{1}{2}$" squares from the background fabric.
- Cut four $4\frac{1}{2}$" squares from the floral fabric.

CENTER MEDALLION

PIECING THE BLOCKS

1. Arrange the blocks as shown in the following diagram. Using a $\frac{1}{4}$" seam allowance, piece the nine blocks for the center medallion. NOTE: There is a slight variation in the orientation of Block 2 and Block 3.

APPLIQUÉ BORDER

The original quilt has ten ovals in the top border, nine ovals in the bottom border, and eight ovals in the side borders. The following instructions are for eight ovals on each side.

CUTTING

- Trace thirty-two ovals on the right side of the fabric using Template I. Add a $3/16$" seam allowance when cutting for appliquéing.
- Cut four 3" x 13" strips from the background fabric.
- Cut four 2" squares from a different fabric for the corner blocks.

APPLIQUÉING THE OVALS

1. Appliqué the ovals end to end as shown in the diagram. Then size the border strips to 2" x $12\frac{1}{2}$". NOTE: The orientation of the ovals is different between the side borders and the top and bottom borders.

PIECING THE BORDER

1. Piece the top and bottom borders to the center medallion pieced blocks.
2. Add the 2" squares to the ends of the side borders.
3. Piece the side borders to the center pieced blocks.

PIECED BORDER

CUTTING

- Trace eighty shapes in the fabric of your choice using Template J.
- Trace eighty shapes from the background fabric using Template K.
- Trace four shapes from Template L. Cut them larger, appliqué, and size back down using the template.
- Appliqué the shapes to the corner triangles using Templates E and F.

PIECING THE BORDER

1. Piece the diamond border. This requires a Y seam. Refer to a basic quiltmaking book for Y seam construction, if needed.
2. Piece together the side borders; then piece together the top and bottom borders.
3. Piece the side borders to the medallion.
4. Add the small corner triangles to the top and bottom borders and piece these strips to the medallion.

5. Add the large corner triangles to complete the border.

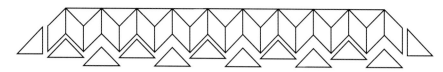

ACCENT BORDER

Measure the center medallion after it is constructed. It should measure $18\frac{1}{2}$" square including seam allowances.

CUTTING

- Cut four $1\frac{1}{4}$" x $18\frac{1}{2}$" border strips.
- Cut four $1\frac{1}{4}$" squares from a contrasting fabric for the corner blocks.

PIECING THE BORDER

1. Piece the side borders to the medallion.
2. Add the corner blocks to the top and bottom borders.
3. Piece the top and bottom borders to the medallion.

The medallion is now complete.

PIECING THE ROWS

The quilt consists of nineteen rows across and nineteen rows down, with the center medallion pieced in the middle. The rows alternate, starting with either a background block or a Variable Star block. Radiating from the corners of the center medallion are twelve blocks that create an X. Four of the blocks within the X are a floral chintz. The middle rows will be pieced in shorter lengths in order to accommodate the center medallion.

1. Arrange the blocks as shown in the diagram.

2. To construct the rows above the center medallion, piece three rows of four stars and three background squares. Piece two rows of four background squares and three stars. Repeat for below.

3. Beginning with a star block row, alternating the beginning block in each subsequent row, piece five rows of these seven blocks to each other. Follow the illustration. Repeat to make a second section.

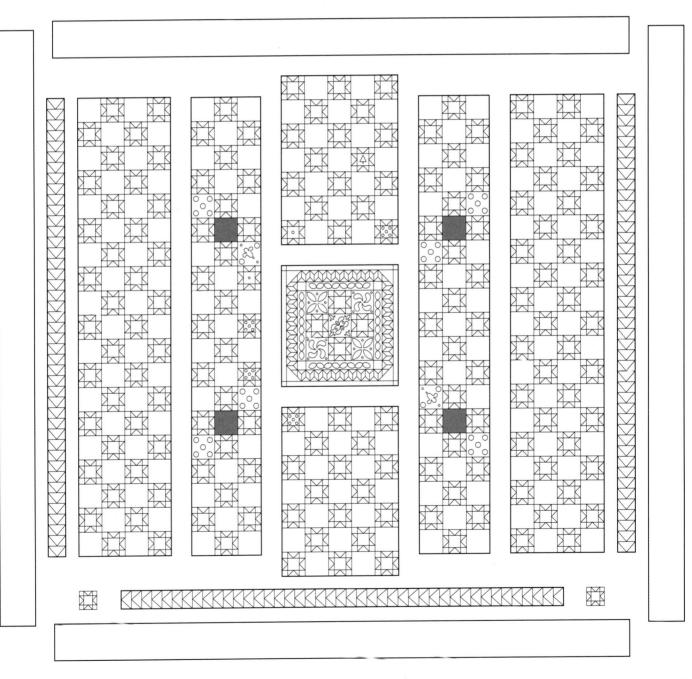

4. Piece one section to the top of the medallion and the other to the bottom of the medallion. Note the orientation of the appliqué blocks.

5. To construct the seven vertical rows pieced on each side of the medallion section, follow the illustration. The appliqué blocks will form the X-shape depicted in the original quilt. This is where the four background squares of floral chintz are used. Alternating the starting block, piece the three rows on either side of the medallion first to each other and then to either side of the medallion section.

6. Repeat the same procedure for the final four rows.

FLYING GEESE BORDER

FLYING GEESE BORDER

The Flying Geese border flies around three sides of the quilt. On the original quilt, the "geese" are larger in the side borders than in the bottom border; the right border has 42 geese, the left border has 43 geese, and the bottom border has 51 geese. The instructions provided give one size for the Flying Geese unit. The original quilt has two 4" Variable Stars pieced in the bottom corners. (If you would like to make only Flying Geese for the border, follow the instructions in parentheses.)

CUTTING

• Cut 132 (136) 4" x 2 1/4" rectangles from your assorted fabrics.
• Cut 264 (272) 2 1/4" squares from the background fabric.

PIECING THE BORDER

1. Refer to the illustrations for piecing the star points on page 94 for piecing the "geese."

2. With right sides together, place a 2 1/4" square on a 2 1/4" x 4" rectangle, with corners matching.

3. Sew from corner to corner.

4. Fold back the square to check for accuracy. Press.

5. Cutting through both layers, trim the excess. Repeat for the other side.

6. Piece into rows of 43 for the sides. Piece one row of 43 (47) for the bottom.

7. Add the side borders to the quilt.

8. Add the two 3 1/2" Variable Stars to the bottom border.

9. Add the bottom border to the quilt.

OUTSIDE BORDER

The outside border is a striped fabric, mitered at the corners.

CUTTING

Measure the length and width through the center of the quilt.

• Cut the top and bottom border strips to measure 5 1/2" wide by the measured length plus 15" for mitering.
• Cut the side borders 5 1/2" wide by the measured length plus 15" for mitering.

PIECING THE BORDER

1. Piece the borders to the quilt top, starting and stopping 1/4" from the corners.

2. To miter the corners, fold the borders right sides together, mark the 45° angle, and sew the seam. Trim to 1/4" and press.

QUILTING

The original quilt was hand quilted with very small, even stitches averaging nine to the inch. Notice there are two quilting patterns for the alternate blocks. Refer to the photo for placement.

1. Turn the quilt top over and press.

2. Mark the quilting designs as shown in the following diagrams.

3. Layer the quilt top, batting, and backing fabric. Baste.

4. Quilt the three layers together.

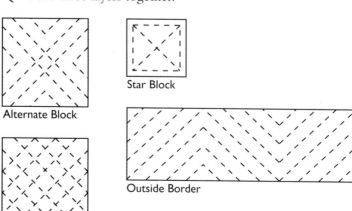

Alternate Block

Star Block

Alternate Block

Outside Border

Detail of *Sarah Johnson* quilt showing maker's initials.

BINDING

The original quilt has a $^1/_8$" self-binding. Yardage for a $^1/_4$"-wide finished, straight-grain, double-fold binding is included in the fabric requirements. This binding will wear better than turning the back to the front as was done on the original quilt.

1. Cut nine 2"-wide strips across the width of the fabric for the binding. Sew the strips together end to end using a diagonal seam. Trim seam allowance to $^1/_4$".

2. Fold and press the strip in half lengthwise. Align the raw edges of the folded strip with the edge of the quilt. Using a $^1/_4$" seam allowance, sew the binding strip to the top of the quilt. Bring the folded edge of the binding strip to the back of the quilt and stitch it down.

3. Add a label with your name, address, name of the quilt, year the quilt was completed, and any other important information.

TEMPLATES

Templates do not include seam allowances.

Appliqué Templates

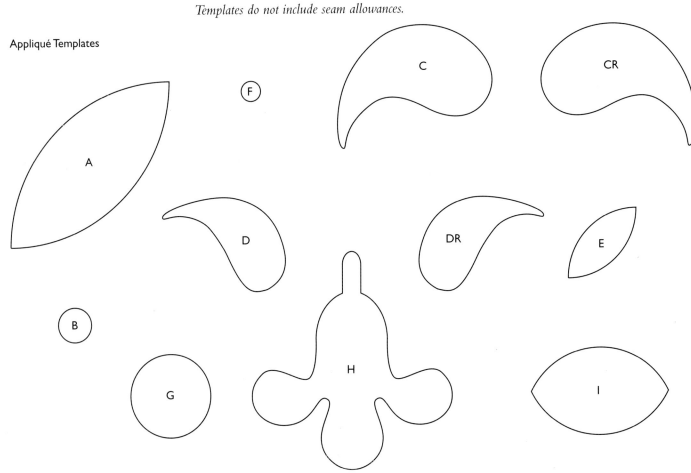

Templates do not include seam allowances.

Templates for Pieced Center Medallion Border

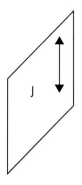

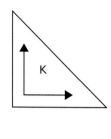

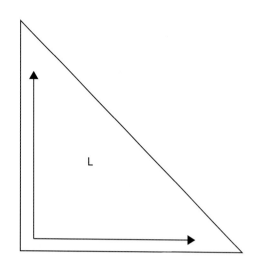

4" Variable Star Templates for hand piecing

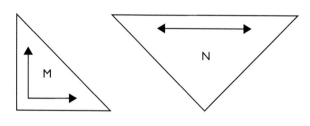

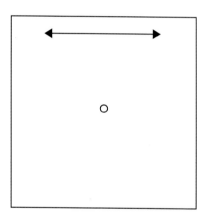

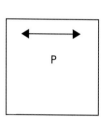

Flying Geese Border Templates for hand piecing

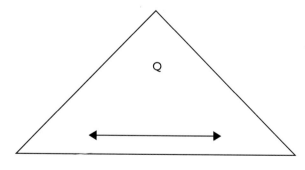

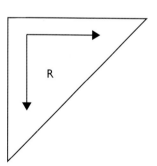

3 1/2" Variable Star Templates for corners of Flying Geese Border

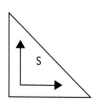

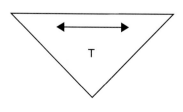

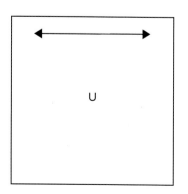

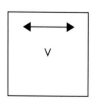

THE PINCUSHION QUILT

Florence Peto illustrated and described this quilt in her book *American Quilts and Coverlets:* "All geometric piecing demanded neatness, with even and well-defined points and angles ... devotees of pieced work will appreciate the dexterity displayed in assembling the Pincushion. When seaming was done with curved lines it took infinite patience, for puckers kept a quilt top from laying flat. Dark but glowing calicoes, ginghams, and chintzes form the pincushions whose concave and convex curves fit into each other with snug precision."[4] The fabrics used in this quilt include roller printed ombré blue and glazed floral chintz with pink roses on a blue ground.

According to New York Census records, eleven Vanderbilt families lived in Clarkston, Rockland County, in the 1830s and 1840s.

The *Pincushion* quilt is a beautiful example of a mid-nineteenth-century scrap quilt. It resembles a pieced version of the Cathedral Window design. The quilt is full of richly-colored prints including calicoes, ginghams, and chintzes. The butter-nut dyed muslin is also the quilt backing; it offers a lovely contrast to the printed fabric and shows off the outline quilting. Framing the center section are three borders. Between two bright, glazed chintz borders is a Flying Geese border whose straight angles offer an excellent contrast to the curves of the "pincushions."

Because this is a scrap quilt, "matching" colors is not necessary. A good combination of dark but vivid fabrics will produce outstanding results. The challenge of this design is piecing the concave and convex curves into each other so they lie flat. Precision of the templates will aid the process considerably. Choose a quilting design that complements the Pincushions and Flying Geese. In the original quilt, diamonds are quilted the length of the outside border and clamshells are quilted the length of the inside borders. Contrasting curves with straight lines not only in piecing, but also in quilting, adds to the quilt's overall striking effect.

The following instructions are a close rendering of the original *Pincushion* quilt and yield a 92 1/2" x 75" quilt with three-hundred forty-five 5" Pincushions, a 2 3/4"-wide Flying Geese border, and two chintz borders. Adapt the pattern or size of the quilt as you wish. This quilt makes a lovely wallhanging as well as a spectacular bed quilt. Because each block is interdependent upon the ones adjacent to it, not every block needs to be pieced in full. A guide identifying how many complete and partial Pincushions you need is provided. Hand-piecing is recommended.

SUPPLIES

Use a variety of dark, vivid fabrics for the Pincushion centers and a light background fabric for the melons and Flying Geese. The fabric requirements below give the total yardage needed.

> 5 1/2 yards background fabric for the melons and Flying Geese border
> 9 1/2 yards assorted fabrics for the Pincushion centers and Flying Geese
> 2 1/2 yards chintz for the two borders and the binding
> 5 1/2 yards backing fabric
> thin cotton batting

PINCUSHIONS

CUTTING

Trace around the template on the wrong side of the fabric. For accuracy in piecing, mark dots on the back of the fabric at the points and mid-points marked on the templates.

- Trace 345 Pincushions (A), 53 half-Pincushions (C), and 2 quarter-Pincushions (D) from various fabrics, adding a 1/4" seam allowance when cutting. Position the template on the fabric matching the arrow to the grain of the fabric. This piece lies flat when pieced if the grainline is the same as on the melons. Mark the ends and midpoints.

- Trace 744 melons (B) from the background fabric, adding a 1/4" seam allowance when cutting. Position the template on the fabric matching the arrow to the grain of the fabric. This piece lies flat when pieced if the grainline is the same as on the Pincushions. Mark the ends and midpoints.

Pieced Quilt, Pincushion Pattern. 1850-1860.

Made by a member of the Vanderbilt family.

Rockland County, New York. Cotton.

95" x 80". Museum acquisition 1955-676.

(10-164)

Templates do not include seam allowances.

Need 744

B

mid-point

A

Need 345

Need 53

C

D   Need 2

HAND PIECING THE PINCUSHIONS

1. Align the reference marks and pin.
2. Hand piece the melons and the Pincushion centers together.
3. Follow the diagram below for piecing. You will need 15 complete Pincushions (Block 1), 308 Pincushions with two melons attached (Block 2), 22 Pincushions with three melons attached (Block 3), 53 half-Pincushions (Block 4), and 2 corners (Block 5).

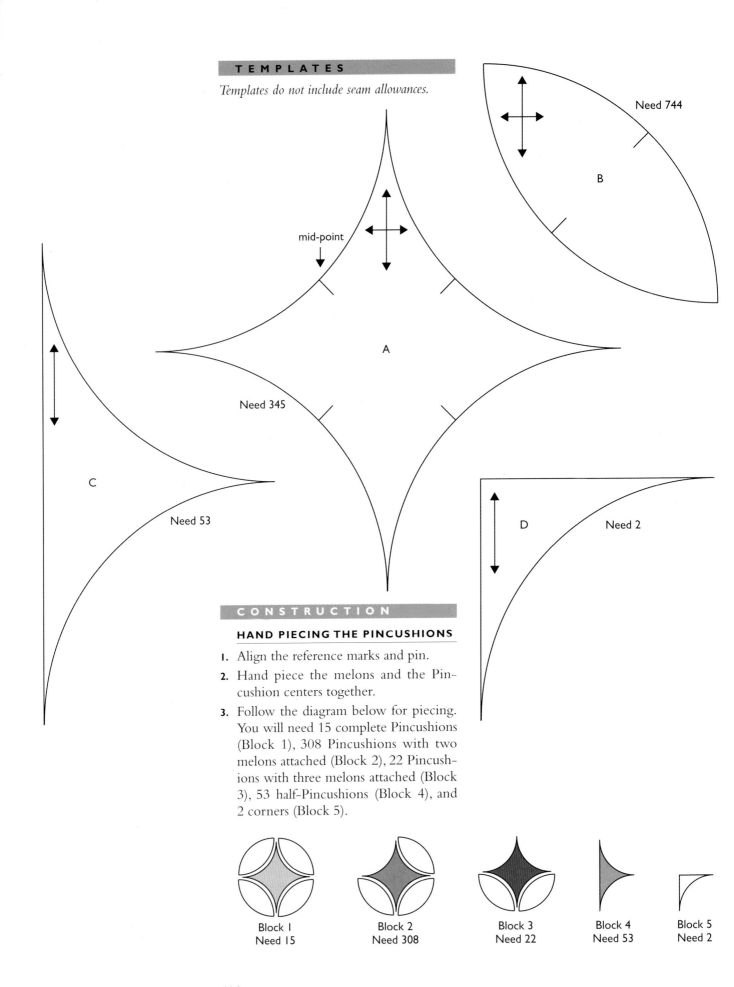

Block I
Need 15

Block 2
Need 308

Block 3
Need 22

Block 4
Need 53

Block 5
Need 2

ASSEMBLING THE ROWS

1. Arrange the Pincushions into rows as shown in the diagram at the right.
2. Hand piece the rows together.

CUTTING

Measure the length and width through the center of the quilt.

- Cut two strips for the side borders 3¼" wide by the measured length plus 11" for mitering.
- Cut two strips for the top and bottom border 3¼" by the measured width plus 11" for mitering.

PIECING THE INSIDE BORDER

1. Using a ¼" seam allowance, piece the borders to the quilt. Start and stop ¼" from the corners to allow for mitering.
2. To miter the corners, fold the borders right sides together, mark the 45° angle, and sew the seam. Trim to ¼" and press.

Detail of *Pincushion* quilt

FLYING GEESE BORDER

CUTTING

- Cut 186 "geese" from Template E. (Or cut 47 4½" squares and cut into quarters diagonally.*)
- Cut 372 background triangles from Template F. (Or cut 186 2½" squares and cut into half diagonally.*)

*This method includes seam allowance.

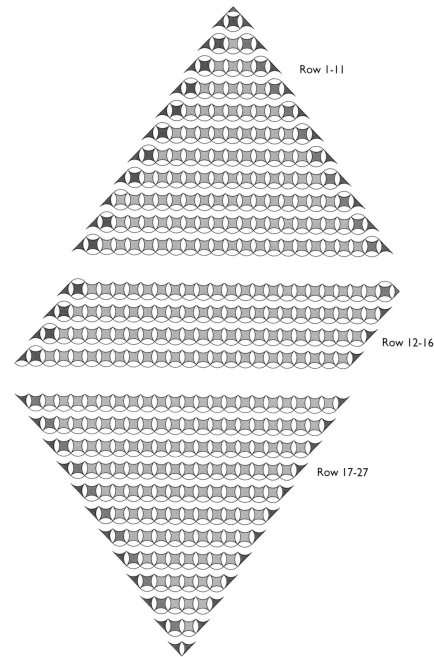

Row 1-11

Row 12-16

Row 17-27

TEMPLATES

Templates do not include seam allowances.

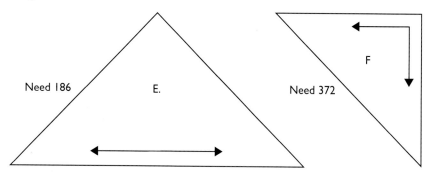

Need 186

E.

F

Need 372

PIECING THE FLYING GEESE UNITS

1. Pair two F triangles with one E triangle.
2. Follow the diagram below for piecing the Flying Geese unit.

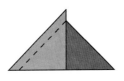

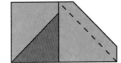

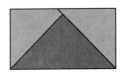

3. Piece strips of 41 "geese" for the top and bottom borders and 56 "geese" for the side borders.
4. Adjust the Flying Geese border if necessary.
5. Using a ¹/₄" seam allowance, piece the top and bottom borders to the quilt.
6. Piece the side borders to the quilt.
7. Press.

OUTSIDE CHINTZ BORDER

CUTTING

Measure the length and width through the center of the quilt.

- Cut two strips for the side borders 2¹/₂" wide by the measured length plus 9" for mitering.
- Cut two strips for the top and bottom border 2¹/₂" wide by the measured width plus 9" for mitering.

PIECING THE OUTSIDE BORDER

1. Using a ¹/₄" seam allowance, piece the chintz border strips to the Flying Geese border. Start and stop ¹/₄" from the corners to allow for mitering.
2. To miter the corners, fold the borders right sides together, mark the 45° angle, and sew the seam. Trim to ¹/₄" and press.

QUILTING

1. Mark the top for quilting as shown in the diagrams below.
2. Layer the quilt top, batting, and backing. Baste.
3. Quilt the three layers together.

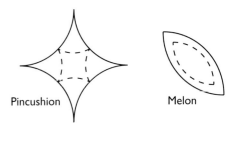

Pincushion   Melon

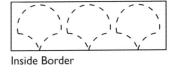

Inside Border

Outside Border

BINDING

Yardage for a ¹/₄"-wide finished, straight-grain, double-fold binding is included in the fabric requirements for the chintz. This type of binding will wear better than turning the back to the front as was done on the original quilt.

1. Cut nine 2"-wide strips across the width of the fabric for the binding. Sew the strips together end to end using a diagonal seam. Trim seam allowance to ¹/₄".
2. Fold and press the strip in half lengthwise. Align the raw edges of the folded strip with the edge of the quilt. Using a ¹/₄" seam allowance, sew the binding strip to the top of the quilt. Bring the folded edge of the binding strip to the back of the quilt and stitch it down.
3. Add a label with your name, address, name of the quilt, year the quilt was completed, and any other important information.

End Notes

Electra Havemeyer Webb and The Shelburne Museum

1 For a complete discussion on the Havemeyers and their collections, see *Splendid Legacy: The Havemeyer Collection* (New York: Metropolitan Museum of Art, 1993). See also Frances Weitzenhoffer's *The Havemeyers: Impressionism Comes to America* (New York: Harry N. Abrams, 1986).

2 Electra H. Webb, "Americana at Shelburne," East Side House Winter Antique Show (New York, 1957).

3 Electra H. Webb, "The Shelburne Museum and How It Grew," unpublished speech delivered at Colonial Williamsburg, Williamsburg, Virginia (January 30, 1958), 6.

4 Letter from Electra H. Webb to Louis C. Jones, New York State Historical Association at Cooperstown, dated Oct. 10, 1949.

5 Florence Peto, *American Quilts and Coverlets* (New York: Chanticleer Press, 1949); and *Historic Quilts* (New York: The American Historical Co., 1939).

6 Electra H. Webb, "Folk Art in Shelburne Museum," *Art in America*, 43:2, (May 1955), 63.

7 Aline B. Saarinen, *The Proud Possessors* (New York: Random House, 1958), 297.

8 Webb, "The Shelburne Museum and How It Grew," 22.

American Quilts in the Home

1 Probate Record, Salmon Dutton, 1824, Windsor County Records, Springfield, Vermont.

2 See Abbott Lowell Cummings, *Bed Hangings: A Treatise on Fabrics and Styles in the Curtaining of Beds 1650-1850* (Boston, MA: The Society for the Preservation of New England Antiquities, 1961).

3 From Thomas Malton, *A Compleat Treatise on Perspective*, Second Edition (London, 1778), Plate 34. Winterthur Museum Library.

4 *The Workwoman's Guide by a Lady* (London: Simpkin, Marshall, & Co., 1838; CT: Opus Publications with Sturbridge Village), 198-200. See also Elisabeth Donaghy Garrett, *At Home: The American Family 1750-1870* (New York: Harry N. Abrams, Inc., 1990).

5 Parts of this paper have been adapted from an essay by the author entitled "For Warmth and Beauty: Bedcovers and Bedchambers in America," included in the exhibition catalogue *Quilts from the Shelburne Museum* (Tokyo: Kokusai Art, 1996).

6 William Chauncey Langdon, *Everyday Things in American Life* 1607-1776 (New York: Charles Scribner's Sons, 1946), 50.

7 As quoted in Lyn A. Bonfield, "The Production of Cloth, Clothing and Quilts in 19th Century New England Homes," *Uncoverings* 1981 (Mill Valley, CA: American Quilt Study Group, 1982), 82.

8 This paper focuses primarily on the textiles produced in English settlements in the New World. See also John Irwin and Katharine B. Brett, *Origins of Chintz* (London: Her Majesty's Stationery Office, 1970); Schnuppe von Gwinner, *The History of the Patchwork Quilt* (West Chester, PA: Schiffer Publishing, 1988); *Die Geschichte des Patchwork Quilts* (Munich: Keyser Publishing, Ltd., 1987).

9 Bernard Bailyn, *The New England Merchants in the 17th Century* (NY: Harper and Row, 1964), 72; as quoted in Linda R. Baumgarten, "The Textile Trade in Boston, 1650-1700" in *Arts of the Anglo-American Community in the Seventeenth Century*, ed. by Ian M.G. Quimby, Winterthur Conference Report, 1974 (Winterthur, Delaware: Henry Francis du Pont Winterthur Museum & University of Virginia, Charlottesville), 220.

10 Camlet is a medium-weight fabric made of worsted yarns, wool and worsted, and/or worsted and silk and woven in stripes, checks, spots, changeable and brocaded patterns; serge is a medium-weight twilled cloth woven with a worsted wool warp and woolen weft. As described by Florence Montgomery in *Textiles in America, 1650-1870* (New York: W. W. Norton & Co., 1984).

11 Gloria Seaman Allen, *First Flowerings: Early Virginia Quilts* (Washington, DC: DAR Museum, 1987), 9.

12 See also Florence M. Montgomery, *Printed Textiles: English and American Cottons and Linens, 1700-1850* (New York: Viking Press, 1970), 17-18.

13 C. J. H. Woodbury, "Textile Education Among the Puritans," reprinted from the *The Bulletin of the National Association of Wool Manufacturers, June 1911* (Boston Office, 683 Atlantic Ave, 1911). Catherine Fennelly, *Textiles in New England, 1790-1840* (Sturbridge, Massachusetts: Old Sturbridge Village), 9.

14 As quoted in Jane Nylander, *Our Own Snug Fireside: Images of the New England Home 1760-1860* (New York: Alfred A. Knopf, 1993), 61.

15 See also Abbott Lowell Cummings, *Bed Hangings: A Treatise on Fabrics and Styles in the Curtaining of Beds 1650-1850* (Boston, MA: The Society for the Preservation of New England Antiquities, 1961).

16 Gloria Seaman Allen, "Quiltmaking on Chesapeake Plantations," *On the Cutting Edge: Textile Collectors, Collections, and Traditions* (Lewisburg, PA: Oral Traditions, 1994), 57-59.

17 Gloria Seaman Allen, *First Flowerings: Early Virginia Quilts* (Washington, DC: DAR Museum), 6.

18 Sarah Emery, *Memories of an Octagenerian,* as quoted in Garrett, *At Home: The American Family, 1750-1850,* 115.

19 Peter Floud, *The Magazine Antiques,* Nov. 1957, 456-459. Reportedly, this quilt was made and used by Mrs. Dutton, who gave it to her daughter, Ann Dutton. The quilt descended through the Dutton family and was presented to the Museum in memory of Frank Jenkins, the last member of that branch of the Dutton family.

20 Mary Louise Benjamin, *A Genealogy of the Family of Lieutenant Samuel Benjamin and Tabitha Livermore, his wife, early settlers of Livermore, Maine* (Winthrop, Maine, 1900). Jonathan Livermore was the fifth generation of Livermores in the United States. He was born in 1729, in Northboro, Massachusetts, and graduated from Harvard College in 1760. He studied for the ministry and became the first pastor of the Congregational Church in Wilton in 1763. He built a house and barn in Wilton, as well as a sawmill on Gambol Brook, in the 1770s, possibly after he resigned from the Church in 1777 because of political differences. He married Elizabeth Kidder of Billerica, Massachusetts, in 1769,

and the couple had ten children. The quilt was passed down through the family to the previous owner, who lives in Reverend Livermore's house.

21 Dorothy Dudley, *The Cambridge of 1776: Wherein Is Set Forth An Account of the Town, And of the Events Witnessed: With Which Is Incorporated The Diary of Dorothy Dudley* (Cambridge, MA, 1876), 78, as quoted in Garrett, *At Home*, 115.

22 Henry Wansey, "An Excursion to the United States of American in the Summer of 1794," (England, 1798), as quoted in Grace Rogers Cooper, *Copp Family Textiles* (Washington, DC: Smithsonian Institution Press, 1971), 20-23; and Cummings, *Bed Hangings*, 31. A set of bed hangings, coverlet, and window curtains in the Copp family collection were handwoven of single-ply linen in a blue-and-white check pattern; see Cooper, *Copp Family Textiles*, 20, 23-24.

23 As quoted in Mary Schoeser and Celia Rufey, *English and American Textiles from 1790 to the Present* (New York: Thames and Hudson, 1989), 30-31.

24 Fennelly, *Textiles in New England, 1790-1840*, 32.

25 Ben Franklin to Deborah Franklin February 19, 1758, as quoted in Garrett, *At Home*, 120.

26 Florence M. Montgomery, *Printed Textiles: English and American Cottons and Linens, 1750-1850*, 31.

27 Kathryn W. Berenson, "Origins and Traditions of Marseilles Needlework," *Uncoverings 1995* (San Francisco, CA: American Quilt Study Group, October 1995), 17.

28 Victoria and Albert Museum, *Notes on Quilting*, 6. This patchwork medallion style went out of fashion in much of England by the nineteenth century, but survived in some rural areas, notably Yorkshire, Durham, and Northumberland as well as South Wales. See also Averil Colby, *Patchwork* (London: B.Batsford, 1976).

29 Ruth E. Finley, *Old Patchwork Quilts and the Women Who Made Them* (Philadelphia, PA: J.B.Lippincott Co., 1929), 165-168.

30 Schoeser and Rufey, *English and American Textiles from 1790 to the Present*, 45.

31 Steponaitus, Louis William, "The Textile Industry in Vermont 1770-1973: Its Development, Diffusion and Decline." Ph.D. Dissertation, University of Vermont, 1976.

32 See also Diane Fagan Affleck, *Just New From the Mills: Printed Cottons in America* (North Andover, MA: Museum of American Textile History, 1987).

33 *Middlebury National Standard*, December 12, 1818.

34 *Middlebury National Standard*, September 24, 1817.

35 *Middlebury National Standard*, October 1, 1817.

36 Irwin and Brett, *Origins of Chintz*, 27.

37 Fennelly, *Textiles in New England, 1790-1840*, 10.

38 James Stuart and Nicolas Revett, *Classical Antiquities of Athens* (London: E. Stuart, 1789; Benjamin Blom, 1968). See also Graham Hood, "Early Neoclassicism in America," *The Magazine Antiques*, 140 (December, 1991) 978-985; and Wendy A. Cooper, *Classical Taste in America 1800-1840* (New York: Abbeville Press and The Baltimore Museum of Art, 1993).

39 Robert Adams, *Works in Architecture and Ruins of the Emperor Diocletian at Spalatro in Dalmatia*, 1764.

40 Gloria Seaman Allen and Nancy G. Tuckhorn, *A Maryland Album: Quiltmaking Traditions, 1634-1934* (Nashville, TN: Rutledge Hill Press, 1995), 41.

41 Schoeser and Rufey, *English and American Textiles*, 42-43.

42 See Gloria Seaman Allen, *First Flowerings: Early Virginia Quilts*, a catalogue published in conjunction with the exhibition at the DAR Museum, which featured numerous quilts made of floral chintz cloth.

43 Fennelly, *Textiles in New England*, 26.

44 *Middlebury National Standard*, November 28, 1828, 4.

45 *Godey's Lady's Book*. vol. 10 (Philadelphia: L. A. Godey, January 1835), 41.

46 Miss Leslie, *The House Book* (Philadelphia: Carey & Hart, 1840), 116.

47 *Godey's Lady's Book*. vol. 39 (Philadephia: L. A. Godey, September 1849), 16.

48 My appreciation to Nancy Tuckhorn, Curator of Quilts, DAR Museum, Washington DC, for sharing her research material on the Maryland Institute Fairs.

49 Pat Ferrero, Elaine Hedges, and Julie Silber, *Hearts and Hands: The Influence of Women and Quilts on American Society* (San Francisco: Quilt Digest Press, 1987), 38.

50 Jonathan Holstein develops this premise in his essay, "The American Block Quilt," *In the Heart of Pennsylvania* (Lewisburg, PA: Oral Traditions, 1986), 16-27.

51 See Helene Von Rosenstiel and Gail Caskey Winkler, *Floor Coverings for Historic Buildings* (Washington, D.C.: The Preservation Press, 1988).

52 See John W. Heisey, *A Checklist of American Coverlet Weavers* (Williamsburg, VA: Abby Aldrich Rockfeller Folk Art Center, Colonial Williamsburg Foundation, 1978). The Checklist identifies and lists information on more than 900 weavers; 67 professional weavers were working in the state of New York.

53 See also Lynn Barber, *The Heyday of Natural History, 1820-1870* (New York: Doubleday & Co., 1980).

54 See Jennifer F. Goldsborough, "Baltimore Album Quilts," *The Magazine Antiques* (March 1994), 412-421; and Dena Katzenberg, *Baltimore Album Quilts* (Baltimore, MD: Baltimore Museum of Art, 1981).

55 Owen Jones, *The Grammar of Ornament* (London: Messrs Day and Son, 1856; London: Studio Editions, 1986).

56 See also Linda Otto Lipsett, *Women and Their Friendship Quilts* (San Francisco, CA: Quilt Digest Press, 1985); and Sandy Fox, *For Purpose and Pleasure: Quilting Together in Nineteenth Century America* (Nashville, TN: Rutledge Hill Press, 1995).

57 My appreciation to Mimi Sherman for sharing her research on Quaker pieced quilts. See Mimi Sherman, "The Fabric of One Family," *The Clarion*, 14:2 (Spring 1989), 55-62.

58 Linda Otto Lipsett, *Pieced from Ellen's Quilt* (Ohio: Halstead and Meadows Publishing, 1991), 201.

59 Miss Leslie, *The House Book*, 116.

60 See Sally Garroute, "Marseilles Quilts and their Offspring," *Quiltmaking in America: Beyond the Myths*, (Nashville, TN: Rutledge Hill Press, 1994), 71-79; and Kathryn W. Berenson, "Origins and Traditions of Marseilles Needlework" *Uncoverings 1995* (San Francisco: American Quilt Study Group, 1995), 7-32.

61 Eileen and Richard Dubrow, *Furniture Made in America 1875-1905* (Exton, PA: Schiffer Publishing, Ltd., 1982), 300.

62 Eastlake, *Hints on Household Taste: The Classic Handbook of Victorian Interior Decoration*, 167.

63 Oscar P. Fitzgerald, *Three Centuries of American Furniture* (New York: Gramercy Publishing Co. 1982), 251.

64 Charles E. Eastlake, *Hints on Household Taste: The Classic Handbook of Victorian Interior Decoration* (London: Longmans, Green and Co., 1878; New York: Dover, 1969), 40.

65 F. A. Moreland, *The Curtain-maker's Handbook: A Reprint of Practical Decorative Upholstery* (Reprint of 1889 publication; New York: E. P. Dutton, 1979), 23; Schoesser and Rufey, *English and American Textiles*, 105, as quoted in Eastlake, *Hints on Household Taste*, 100; Mrs. H. W. Beecher, *All around the House: or How to Make a Home Happy* (New York, 1879), 51.

66 Pat Ferrero, Elaine Hedges, and Julie Silber, *Hearts and Hands: The Influence of Women and Quilts on American Society* (San Francisco: Quilt Digest Press, 1987), 94.

67 Dubrow, *Furniture Made in America 1875-1905*, 257.

68 *Pieced from Ellen's Quilt*, 29.

69 *Godey's Lady's Book* (December 1887) as quoted in Virginia Gunn, "Crazy Quilts and Outline Quilts: Popular Responses to Decorative Art/Needlework Movement, 1876-1893," *Uncoverings, 1984* (Mill Valley, CA: American Quilt Study Group, 1985), 146.

70 Penny McMorris and Micheal Kile, *The Art Quilt* (San Francisco: Quilt Digest Press, 1986), 31.

71 Roderick Kiracofe, *The American Quilt: A History of Cloth and Comfort 1750-1950* (New York: Clarkson Potter, 1993), 173.

72 Patsy and Myron Orlofsky, *Quilts in America* (New York: McGraw Hill, 1974), 222.

73 Barbara Brackman, *Clues in Calico: A Guide to Identifying and Dating Antique Quilts* (McLean, VA: EPM Publications, Inc.,1989), 170.

74 Carrie A. Hall and Rose G. Kretsinger, *The Romance of the Patchwork Quilt in America.* (New York: Bonanza Books, 1935), 40.

75 My appreciation to Merikay Waldvogel for bringing this pattern book to my attention.

76 Collection of Abby Aldrich Rockefeller Folk Art Center #78.608.1

77 David Burne et al, *An American Portrait: A History of the United States* (New York: Charles Scribner's Sons, 1948), 523.

78 Alice Winchester, ed., *Living with Antiques* (New York: Robert M. McBride & Co., 1922). See also Introduction by Kenneth Ames, *The Colonial Revival in America*, ed. Alan Axelrod (New York: W. W. Norton &

Co. for Henry Francis du Pont Winterthur Museum, 1985).

79 Cuesta Benberry, "First Quilt Revival. Part II," *Quilter's Newsletter Magazine* (September 1979), 25, as quoted in Kiracofe, *The American Quilt*, 210.

80 Carrie A. Hall and Rose G. Kretsinger, *The Romance of the Patchwork Quilt in America* (Caldwell, ID: Caxton Printers, 1935), 29.

81 Ibid.

82 Joyce Gross, "Four Twentieth-Century Quiltmakers," AQSG, *Quiltmaking in America: Beyond the Myths* (Nashville, Tennessee: Rutledge Hill Press, 1994).

83 Marie D. Webster, *Quilts: Their Story and How to Make Them* (New York: Tudor Publishing Company, 1915), 72.

84 My appreciation to Janet Haubrich for the following reference: Margaret MacGregor Magie, "The Disappointed Sculptress," *The Winnetka Fortnightly* (January 24, 1968).

85 *Quilter's Journal*, Fall 1981, Vol. 4, No. 3.

Gallery

1 Ruth Finley, *Old Patchwork Quilts and the Women Who Made Them*, 1929, 165-168.

2 Barbara Morris, "English Printed Textiles," *The Magazine Antiques* (September 1957), 253.

3 Hemenway, *Abby Maria, Vermont Historical Gazetteer*, Vol. II, 596, 611.

4 This quilt closely resembles a quilt signed "Emeline Barker #7," now in the collection of the Museum of the City of New York. The Compass patterns in both quilts are identical and the quilting patterns are also quite similar. The maker did, however, incorporate a variation of the Hickory Leaf pattern for the intermediary appliqué design. (My appreciation to Deborah Ash for sharing her research with me.)

5 Florence Peto, *American Quilts and Coverlets* (New York: Chanticleer Press, 1949), 26-27.

6 Col. Henry G. Noyes and Hariette G. Noyes, *Genealogical Record of some of the Noyes Descendants of James, Nicholas, and Peter Noyes* (Boston, Henry Noyes, 1904), Vol. II, 163.

7 Letter from George Fisher to Willie and George, Stockport, New York, February 29, 1888.

8 Henry Hilliard Earl and Frederick M. Peck, *Fall River and its Industries*, (New York: Atlantic Publishing and Engraving, 1877).

Projects

1 Abby Maria Hemenway, *Vermont Historical Gazetteer* (Burlington, Vermont: A. M. Hemenway, 1871), IV, 690.

2 Letter from Florence Peto to Lilian Carlisle, November 15, 1952, Shelburne Museum Archives.

3 For further information, see Nancy Gibson Tuckhorn, "The Assimilation of German Folk Designs on Maryland Quilts," *The Magazine Antiques* (February 1996), 304-313.

4 Florence Peto, *American Quilts and Coverlets*, 26.

Celia Y. Oliver

CURATOR OF TEXTILES, SHELBURNE MUSEUM, SHELBURNE, VERMONT

As Curator of the Textiles Collections at the Shelburne Museum, Celia Oliver supervises the research, exhibition, and publication of the quilt and bedcover collection, which numbers over six hundred pieces. Recognized as one of the largest and most important quilt collections in the United States, it illustrates the range of needlework, construction techniques, and patterns used in the eighteenth- and nineteenth-century quilting traditions. A recent exhibition, Cloth at Hand: Quilts and Costumes in 19th Century America, examined how technological changes in textile production affected the types of fabric used in fashionable quilts and costumes.

Mrs. Oliver's publications include *55 Famous Quilts from the Shelburne Museum*, "A Quilt Collector's Primer" in *America's Glorious Quilts*, "Electra Havemeyer Webb: Quilts at the Shelburne Museum" in *On the Cutting Edge*, and *Quilts from the Shelburne Museum*, an exhibition catalogue by Kokusai Art.

ACKNOWLEDGMENTS

Many people have contributed to the completion of this book. I would like to extend my heartfelt thanks to them all: First and foremost, to the collectors and donors who have entrusted their heirloom quilts to Shelburne Museum and made their research available. To Todd Hensley at C&T Publishing, Lee Jonsson for her editorial expertise, and all others who worked on its publication. To my colleagues at Shelburne Museum: Brian Alexander for approving the project; Mare Richards and Sloane Stephens for their editorial assistance; Ken Burris for his exceptional photography; Erica Donnis and Betsy Goeke for their research efforts; Barbara McMurray, Conservation Technician; Pauline Mitchell, Registrar; and especially Eloise Beil, Director of Collections, for her day-to-day encouragement, thoughtful commentary, advice, and editorial assistance. To Lilian Baker Carlisle, whose years of research at Shelburne Museum provided the foundation for all subsequent work on the quilt collection. To Nancy Gibson Tuckhorn, Daughters of the American Republic Museum, Washington, D.C., for sharing her expertise, research, and editorial advice. To friends and colleagues who have answered questions and directed me to other sources: Shelly Zegart; Joyce Gross; Merikay Waldvogel; Cuesta Benberry; Barbara Brackman; Julie Silber; Gloria Seaman Allen; Jane K. Hutchins; Mimi Sherman; Deborah Ash; Richard Cleveland and Carolyn Fernandez, Vermont Quilt Festival, Northfield, Vermont; Jeanette Lasansky, Oral Traditions Project, Lewisburg, Pennsylvania; and Diane Fagan Affleck, Museum of American Textile History, Lowell, Massachusetts. And, most of all, to my husband Richard and daughter Nora, for their love, patience, support, and good humor.

Thank you.

Froncie Hoffhine Quinn

PROJECT RESEARCH FOR *ENDURING GRACE*
OWNER, HOOPLA, ESSEX JUNCTION, VERMONT

Froncie Quinn grew up in Bexley, Ohio, but began her quilting career in and around Amish country, where she was taught traditional methods of quiltmaking. Wanting to keep these "hand-done" methods alive, Froncie began teaching her own classes. Her lesson booklets have since developed into the pattern packets that are part of her business today.

Froncie owns and operates Hoopla, a business which produces non-slip tin quilting templates for hand and machine quilters, and she specializes in miniature pattern designs.

She is a juried member of The Vermont Hand Crafters and has been published in several issues of *Miniature Quilt Magazine*.

Froncie lives in Vermont with her husband Mike and their two daughters.

ACKNOWLEDGMENTS

I would like to thank my husband Mike, and girls Sarah and Elizabeth, for "gracefully enduring" the strenuousness of this project. Their unending support and encouragement has afforded me the opportunity to grow and stretch as a person. I am eternally grateful.

I would also like to thank Shelburne Museum, with special recognition to Mare Richards, for trusting me with the gorgeous quilts. It has been a thrill. Their generosity has made this project possible.

My appreciation also goes to Mary Beery of the Clothesline in Dayton, Virginia, for the many consultations that took so much of her time. Her advice has been invaluable.

Lastly, I would like to thank Diana Roberts and John Cram of C&T for their professional advice and for patiently teaching me that the editing process is more than one rewrite.

Other fine books from C&T Publishing

For more information write for a free catalog from:
C&T Publishing, P.O. Box 1456, Lafayette, CA 94549
(800) 284-1114

For fabric and quilting supplies:
Cotton Patch Mail Order
3405 Hall Lane, Dept. CTB, Lafayette, CA 94549
email: cottonpa@aol.com
(800) 835-4418 (510) 283-7883